Walking Toward Christmas

Devotions for Advent

Eric Dean Patterson

*For my sister Cari Beth and her family,
Geoff, Tristan, and Caleb.*

WALKING TOWARD CHRISTMAS: DEVOTIONS FOR ADVENT.
Copyright ©2011 by Eric Dean Patterson. All rights reserved. Printed in the United States of America. No part of this book may be used or reproduced in any manner without the prior written permission of the author.

All Biblical references are taken from the New International Version.

THIRD EDITION.

ISBN: 1440461503.

Contents

Preface

Chapter 1	The Flight to Egypt	1
Chapter 2	Anna and Simeon	5
Chapter 3	The Dedication of Jesus	11
Chapter 4	Aunt, Mentor, Friend	15
Chapter 5	Herod the Great	19
Chapter 6	Jesus the Servant	25
Chapter 7	The Unexpected Christ	29
Chapter 8	Shepherds Keeping Watch	33
Chapter 9	What's in a Name?	37
Chapter 10	Jesus of Biloxi	41
Chapter 11	The Light of the World	47
Chapter 12	The Visitation of the Magi	51
Chapter 13	The Magnificat	57
Chapter 14	The Second Adam	63
Chapter 15	Zechariah's Prophecy and God's Mercy	67
Chapter 16	The Genealogies of the Christ	73

Chapter 17	The Consolation of Israel	79
Chapter 18	Mary: Heroic and Human	83
Chapter 19	Joseph the Dreamer	87
Chapter 20	House of Bread	93
Chapter 21	The Historical Authenticity of Christmas	99
Chapter 22	Christmas is for Everyone	103
Chapter 23	Doubt and Obedience	107
Chapter 24	Troubled Jerusalem	113
Chapter 25	God with Us	117
Reflection Questions		122

Preface

I love Christmas. I wrote this book in order to have a short set of daily Bible studies for the month of Advent. The "walk toward Christmas" is intended to be one of reflection and learning.

Previously, I found Christmas to be a spiritually passé time. In contrast to the discipline and depth of Lent, the penance and promise of Good Friday, and the earth-shaking joy of Easter, my own experience is the spiritual blahs during Christmas.

In discussing this with friends and family, a common refrain was that personal busy-ness and ritual attendance at numerous holiday events (e.g. town tree lighting, a half-dozen church and school "programs," etc.) numbed us to Christmas.

But that was not all. Many of us were relying on our childhood memories and emotional content to dictate how we assessed the quality of Christmas-time. "It doesn't feel like Christmas this year…" And when we substituted a feeling of Christmas for spiritual growth, then the holiday was not only stale—it was lifeless.

Hence, this book. I was challenged to slow down and really read the Biblical Christmas passages in short segments, following the cross-reference verses in the margins of my study Bible. I began to take notes and forced myself to a meditative pace, reflecting on verses and sentences instead of blasting through the story in a couple of days as I had in the past. Like most Christians, I had a wealth of old information from past sermons, Sunday School classes, and a university bachelor's degree in Biblical Studies tucked into my brain to help reawaken my curiosity, once I had committed to slowing down, reflecting, and writing notes every day.

The result, after on-again/off-again writing over parts of three years, is *Walking Toward Christmas*. I dedicate this book to my sister Cari Beth and her family. She and I share fond childhood memories of family Christmas and numerous "closet discussions" about life. I acknowledge and am grateful for the encouragement of my beloved wife Mary in the preparation of this book. I appreciate the assistance of my mother, Dwayla, in developing the reflection questions. Furthermore, I am thankful to the dozens of first-readers who provided feedback and support for the project. Finally, I learned and was challenged by scripture reading and meditation in the process of completing the book, and I hope that you will be also.

Eric Dean Patterson

Chapter 1

The Flight to Egypt

When the Magi had gone, an angel of the Lord appeared to Joseph in a dream. "Get up," he said, "take the child and his mother and escape to Egypt. Stay there until I tell you, for Herod is going to search for the child to kill him." So he got up, took the child and his mother during the night and left for Egypt, where he stayed until the death of Herod…After Herod died, an angel of the Lord appeared in a dream to Joseph in Egypt and said, "Get up, take the child and his mother and go to the land of Israel, for those who were trying to take the child's life are dead."
Matthew 2:13-15, 19-21

Soon after the Magi visited and offered their gifts of gold, frankincense, and myrrh, Joseph was warned of impending catastrophe for his young family: King Herod, known for his efficient ruthlessness, had ascertained the general location of the Christ child and was preparing death squads to eliminate a potential rival to his throne. That Herod had the capacity to kill mercilessly was well-known: he had murdered his way to the Jewish throne and was responsible for the execution of many high-ranking Jews as well as his own wife Mariamne and some of his sons.

Joseph responded immediately, waking Mary, gathering their few belongings, and hastening into the night, bound for Egypt as directed by the angel. The night into which they vanished was both real and figurative. Herod was left in the dark, stymied in his effort to kill the babe. The Light of the World, the Christ, had left Israel, as Joseph shielded the new baby from the world's attention.

They were directed southward to Egypt, an entirely separate jurisdiction that had only recently been made part of the Roman Empire. Egypt has rich Biblical connotations as a place of temporal and temporary succor. It is also historically a place of temptation for the Jews, a place where they could forget the Promised Land of their forefathers and the unique spiritual devotion that they were called to.

Many Old Testament figures found refuge in Egypt. Abram went there with his wife Sarai and left with a fortune. Abram later turned to an Egyptian servant girl in order to sire an heir. Decades later his grandson Jacob found relief from famine in Egypt and Jacob's son Joseph rose to the prime minister's position, saving Egypt and its people from seven years of deadly famine. Moses became a prince of Egypt when lost to his parents, and the Jewish nation thrived for four centuries in the incubator of Egypt prior to the events leading to the Exodus. Solomon cemented his grandest political alliance by marrying Pharaoh's daughter and built his army around 12,000 of Egypt's finest steeds. Later kings would side with Egypt in regional power politics and Egypt became a haven for Jewish refugees fleeing Assyrians, Babylonians, and Seleucids over the centuries.

Thus it was natural for Joseph and Mary to head to Egypt, and the most logical destination for them in Egypt was Alexandria. This city, founded by Alexander the Great in 332 B.C., was known throughout the world for its love of learning, tolerance for different ideas and customs, and its multitude of schools and massive library. It was also well-known among Jews as the second city of Judaism, boasting a Jewish population larger than that of Jerusalem which exercised quasi-independent self-government in two of the city's five districts. It was at Alexandria that the Septuagint, the Greek version of the Old Testament, was translated circa 300-200 B.C. and many of Judaism's great philosophers, most notably Philo, resided in Alexandria.

Nonetheless, Egypt was problematic because it was a tempting final destination rather than a mere way-stop. God's plan was for Egypt to only be a temporary refuge for his people: Abram left and returned to Canaan, Jacob prophesied that his descendants would return to the Promised Land and Moses fulfilled that by leading the Israelites out of Egypt. Centuries later, the Alexandria Diaspora felt so comfortable in Egypt that they built their own temple there. However, God never meant for Egypt to be his people's final destination—the time spent there was only to be temporary as it merely provided short term, material refuge.

Egypt was a place of material well-being, but not one of spiritual well-being. It was there that Abram lied and caused his wife to live under false and dangerous pretenses, it was there that Joseph's star waxed only after it had waned, and the Egypt of Moses' day was alluring enough that many Israelites longed to return there rather than face the unknown wilderness en route to the Promised Land. Solomon's dalliance with Egypt epitomized spiritual compromise in the area of personal and public well-being. Following Nebuchadnezzar's conquest of Jerusalem, Jeremiah warned the remnant of Jews left in Judah that God did not want them to go to Egypt—but naturally they disobeyed, supporting Egypt in its doomed encounter with Babylon at the Battle of Carchemish. Of course, this disobedience resulted in destruction and slavery for many.

This historical backdrop sets the stage for the temptations that Mary and Joseph may have faced in residing in Egypt. We do not know how long Mary and Joseph remained in Egypt, it could have been months or it could have been several years. During this time they would have integrated into the local Jewish community, made friends and perhaps associated with distant relatives, participated in the local synagogue, and began to operate a successful carpenter's shop. It is possible that over time they became comfortable in Egypt, and that the thought of a major move back across the Negev to Judea or Galilee with Jesus and perhaps their other small children was unpalatable.

From a financial standpoint, it is entirely possible that Egypt provided them with a better opportunity for stability, security, and making a living than did the Palestinian backwater of the Roman Empire that was politically unstable, economically depressed, and ultimately convulsed by civil war and mass destruction a few decades later. In contrast to all this, Egypt appeared to be prosperous and secure. Moreover, Mary and Joseph may have even wondered if their son would repeat the Joseph story all over again, rising to prominence in Egypt and then saving all of Israel as a sort of Joseph- or Moses-type hero.

In short, although they may have missed home in Israel, it is just as likely that they had settled into a Jewish expatriate community in Egypt and were flourishing therein.

Some time later, probably several years following the desperate pre-dawn escape to Egypt, the angel returned and bid Joseph travel back to Israel. To his credit, Joseph obeyed once again, leaving the temporary material security enjoyed in Egypt and leading his family with some uncertainty to a remote part of Palestine. And it is likely that the lessons of parents' obedience and faith were not lost on the growing boy in their household, who himself would forsake material comfort and the possibility of earthly renown to consummate, at great personal sacrifice, redemptive history by his ministry and death. The example of Joseph and Mary should remind us both that God cares for us and will lead our families, as well as that He has a long-term spiritual destiny for each of His children. We do well to be grateful for his blessing in times of plenty, but not mistake fleeting material success for the ultimate spiritual purpose and meaning inherent in our service to Him.

Chapter 2

Anna and Simeon

When the time of their purification according to the Law of Moses had been completed, Joseph and Mary took him to Jerusalem to present him to the Lord (as it is written in the Law of the Lord, "Every firstborn male is to be consecrated to the Lord"), and to offer a sacrifice in keeping with what is said in the Law of the Lord: "a pair of doves or two young pigeons." Now there was a man in Jerusalem called Simeon, who was righteous and devout. He was waiting for the consolation of Israel, and the Holy Spirit was upon him. It had been revealed to him by the Holy Spirit that he would not die before he had seen the Lord's Christ. Moved by the Spirit, he went into the temple courts. When the parents brought in the child Jesus to do for him what the custom of the Law required, Simeon took him in his arms and praised God, saying: "Sovereign Lord, as you have promised, you now dismiss your servant in peace. For my eyes have seen your salvation, which you have prepared in the sight of all people, a light for revelation to the Gentiles and for glory to your people Israel." The child's father and mother marveled at what was said about him. Then Simeon blessed them and said to Mary, his mother: "This child is destined to cause the falling and rising of many in Israel, and to be a sign that will be spoken against, so that the thoughts of many hearts will be revealed. And a sword will pierce your own soul too." There was also a prophetess, Anna, the daughter of Phanuel, of the tribe of Asher. She was very old; she had lived with her husband seven years after her marriage and then was a widow until she was eighty-four. She never left the temple but worshiped night and day, fasting and praying. Coming up to them at that very moment, she gave thanks to God and spoke about the child to all who were looking forward to the redemption of Jerusalem. Luke 2:22-37

This passage suggests again the contradictory nature of Christ's coming in flesh to a fallen world. The setting would have been common for any Jewish family: nearly six weeks after the baby's birth, the parents traveled the five miles from Bethlehem up to the temple in Jerusalem to consecrate their baby. This dedication was detailed in Mosaic law, as Luke points out in this passage.[1] What would have been uncommon is that this trip may have occurred in the midst of ongoing travel associated with Augustus' census. Therefore, the roads and inns continued to be full, and certainly the temple area must have been crowded and noisy, as Jews from far and wide returned to their ancestral land and made the pilgrimage to the temple. This modest family—a humble carpenter, his young wife, and baby child—would have gone largely unnoticed in the throng.

This story demonstrates some of the confusion surrounding the person and ministry of the Messiah. Both Simeon and Anna seemed to expect a national, political Savior. In this they were in good company, as everyone from Herod to the Jewish religious elite expected that the newborn king must be a political figure. Simeon said that Jesus would bring not only salvation but also "glory to...Israel." Anna saw that the child "would cause the rising and falling of many." We do not know if they foresaw the life Christ was to lead or his future millennial kingdom, but both prophetic utterances could lend themselves to a political interpretation: the Messiah as earthly king, one coming to change the political and social order rather than a Savior who came to transform the netherworld of the human heart.

However, their actual words clearly reveal the historical and spiritual Christ as we know him. Simeon said that this baby was the embodiment of God's salvation, "a light for the Gentiles and for glory to your people." This phrase suggests that the Savior would be a revelatory light to the non-Jewish world, bringing universal redemption to humanity. Moreover, Jesus was not

---

[1] Leviticus 12:4-6.

to lead the Jewish people to a glorious position in global political affairs, but rather to bring the glory of God's goodness and salvation to the Jewish population. Probably, Simeon had more prophetic insight into Jesus' future which he shared at the time, because Luke records that Mary and Joseph "marveled" at what Simeon had to say.

Then Simeon blessed the parents, probably offering a prayer that God would give them wisdom, patience, and endurance as new parents to a tiny, demanding babe. Then he turned to Mary with another statement that likely nagged at her heart over the years of Jesus' childhood and adult ministry. Simeon looked her in the eye and said, "This child is destined to cause the falling and rising of many...be a sign that will be spoken against...many hearts will be revealed...and a sword will pierce your own soul too." And then...? Perhaps Simeon hugged them, with tears in his eyes as he began to sense the confrontational ministry that lay ahead of Jesus and the tragedy of betrayal and execution. And then, in the crowded chaos of the temple, this profound stranger slipped off.

If they were marveling at his first words, the parents must have been flabbergasted by his comments to Mary. This baby would reveal the deepest motivations of the human heart and cause the "rising and falling" of many?! What did the old man mean that "a sword will pierce your own soul?" I doubt that Mary and Joseph were expecting such sinister intimations, particularly after having been visited by angels, shepherds, and Magi in the past month. One can imagine Mary pulling close to Joseph with confused tears in her eyes as Joseph tried to soothe her.

And then, another ancient personage accosted them. This time it was a wrinkled old woman, one who had doubled the life expectancy of her day. Anna may have been seen by the temple functionaries as a devout old woman, or she may have been thought of as somewhat crazed by harmless. We do not know. We are told that upon seeing the Christ child, she immediately knew that this was the Messiah and broke out into psalms of thanksgiving, "Glory to God, this is the one, this is the Messiah, thank you Jehovah!"

We do not know exactly what Anna said, but we do know that she began testifying to the people around her. Imagine, a hunched over old woman in modest attire, spontaneously and exuberantly praising God, and stopping the crowd of passerbys to relate to them this incredible news, "This baby...he is the Messiah! This is the Savior! Jehovah has kept his promise! This babe will redeem Israel!"

In the crowded temple, a few may have stopped and listened, particularly those who knew that Anna was spiritually devoted and wise. Others may have taken a glance at the worn, humble attire of the carpenter and his young wife, and moved on. Few could believe that this tiny new baby, born in poverty, would someday have the resources for the "redemption of Israel." That would take a king, a warrior, the very Son of God acting in power as in the days of Moses and Joshua.

Nonetheless, we should not be shocked at the indifference of the people. The passage reminds us that there are some, like Simeon and Anna, who are looking for, waiting for, seeking for God to be lord of their world. Such people are "acceptors" who are listening for God's voice—and ultimately God will speak to them. The Magi, the shepherds, Mary, Joseph, Elisabeth, Zechariah, Simeon, Anna—they were distinguished by their openness to God's leading and their willingness to follow. Thus, the lesson from the lives of Simeon and Anna is that a personal God knows our deepest aspirations and wants to bless our inner person with exactly the kind of fulfillment that only He can provide and which we desperately need. Both Simeon and Anna found that fulfillment and served God by witnessing to that consolation. The question for us is whether we are alert and listening for the voice of God in our life, and whether we are open to not only his will but his way of doing business in our world? It may mean that we witness the "rise and fall" of those around us or even experience pain in our own souls. However, in the end we can have confidence that God has provided that light for all of us in the saving work of Jesus Christ.

Chapter 3

The Dedication of Baby Jesus

When the time of their purification according to the Law of Moses had been completed, Joseph and Mary took him to Jerusalem to present him to the Lord (as it is written in the Law of the Lord, "Every firstborn male is to be consecrated to the Lord"), and to offer a sacrifice in keeping with what is said in the Law of the Lord: "a pair of doves or two young pigeons." Luke 2:22-24

Contemporary readers skim these short verses, moving quickly to the wondrous story of octogenarians appearing out of the temple crowds to bless and prophesy over the baby Christ. However, the actions Joseph and Mary took, and the assumptions underlying the situation, are important symbols rooted in Old Testament history which testify to God's love for humanity and his extreme care in providing redemption to his fallen children. Four themes stand out: covenant, purification, sacrifice, and consecration.

Covenant. At the beginning of recorded history, God made a covenant with Noah, and later established a binding covenant with the Jewish patriarch Abraham.[2] Scholars say that the word for covenant used in these instances is probably derived from the Akkadian verb "to fetter" or "to bind," and parallel usage can be found in other ancient Near Eastern languages.[3] Interestingly, it was the eternal, omnipotent God who took the initia-

---

[2] See Genesis 17.
[3] Vine's Dictionary, p. 50.

tive to engage individual human beings in a binding relationship that imposed obligations on each party.

In the case of Abraham and his descendants, God promised to bless the Jewish nation in perpetuity. The physical sign of that covenant was literally scarred into the flesh of every Jewish male through circumcision. On the first day of the second week following a Jewish male's birth, he was circumcised. Consequently, a few weeks before Joseph and Mary made their way to the temple, baby Jesus was circumcised, just as his antecedents had been for generations before him. This marked him as a child of the covenant, as an heir of all God's promises to Abraham's descendants through Jesus' earthly mother. Of course, the cut of circumcision at the beginning of Jesus' life foreshadowed his bloody death on behalf of the covenant thirty years later.

Purification. Forty days after delivery, the baby boy was to be offered to God by his parents and redeemed with an offering. The interval of five weeks was a time of purification. This was so because the mother was considered ceremonially unclean to venture into the temple area until the appointed forty days had passed, and there was probably a good health rationale for the mother staying close to home in those first weeks. The symbolism of childbirth and purification is important. Giving birth to a baby was certainly not sinful, but the pain associated with childbirth was a reminder of original sin and the chasm that Adam and Eve's sin had caused between God and humanity. The trip to the temple, to the symbolic nexus between God and mankind, and the ensuing ritual of sacrifice and purification symbolized humanity's imperfection and God's gracious cleansing work.

Sacrifice. God claimed as His own every firstborn male in Israel, both man and beast. This was in keeping with his identity as Creator and also as Savior of Israel from bondage. The practice of offering such a sacrifice goes back to the Passover and the Exodus, when God ransomed Israel and took as his "payment" the firstborn in perpetuity.

The procedures of Mary and Joseph's day were simple: take the newborn to the temple in Jerusalem, if possible, and offer a prescribed offering of thanksgiving and redemption. The customary offering was a lamb, however, Mary and Joseph gave a pair of turtledoves or pigeons, indicating their lack of wealth. It is noteworthy that God entrusted the care of his own Son to such a humble pair. Obviously God fully trusted the character and integrity of Mary and Joseph to prepare the boy Jesus for the man he would become.

Consecration. The consummation of these details—the circumcision, purification, ritual sacrifice and accompanying priestly blessing—was an act consecrating the new child as a member of the covenant relationship, and in this case, redeeming the first born upon which God has a special claim. Consecration means to "set aside" for a special purpose, and certainly Christ was ordained for the unique purpose of the Cross. The symbolism of the consecratory moment is rich: the Son of God has entered the world to save it, and his birth is consecrated in a tribute to the great salvation moment in Israel's history, when God struck down the firstborn of Egypt, and the blood of lambs was used as a substitutionary device for atonement. Now, with the birth of Jesus, the final consolation began. A new covenant and a new substitution would take place which absolves mankind of its sin—the death of a firstborn, the Lamb of God, Jesus the Messiah.

Of course, it was impossible for Mary and Joseph to recognize the contours of their baby's future life and ministry as well as all of the symbols implicit in that day. Nonetheless, their simple acts of obedience were steps on a longer journey that led Israel out of captivity in Egypt via blood sacrifice to the ultimate atonement for humankind that would occur at Calvary. And these symbols outline for us the contours of salvation and life commitment God wants from each of his children.

Chapter 4

Aunt, Mentor, Friend

When his [Zechariah] time of service [in the temple] was completed, he returned. After this his wife Elisabeth became pregnant and for five months remained in seclusion. "The Lord has done this for me," she said. "In these days he has shown his favor and taken away my disgrace among the people…Mary…entered Zechariah's home and greeted Elisabeth. When Elisabeth heard Mary's greeting, the baby leaped in her womb, and Elisabeth was filled with the Holy Spirit. In a loud voice she exclaimed: "Blessed are you among women, and blessed is the child you will bear! But why am I so favored that the mother of my Lord should come to me? As soon as the sound of your greeting reached my ears, the boy in my womb leaped for joy. Blessed is she who has believed that what the Lord has said to her will be accomplished!" Luke 1: 23-25, 40-45

Elisabeth was the mother of John the Baptist as well as a confidante, relation, and likely mentor to the mother of Christ. Her important influence on these history-changing people, and the fact that God chose to use her, out of all the Jewish women available in history, should lead us to closer reflection on her life…and ours.

Luke tells us that Elisabeth's husband held important rank as a priest. In contrast, his wife would have carried a stigma in the society of her day. Luke puts it baldly, "she was barren." This candid statement hides depths of shame and inferiority in a society where the primary social role for women was as mother. The Old Testament makes this unenviable position clear in the ridicule experienced by matriarchs such as Sarah, Rachel, and Hannah.

Nevertheless, God chose to bring vitality to the womb of a woman long past her prime, an individual who likely felt resignation at her lot in life. No angel appeared to her, although heavenly messengers foretold the births of Jesus and John to Elisabeth's husband, cousin, and cousin's fiancé. Indeed, Elisabeth apparently learned that something strange was afoot when her husband returned home after a stint working in the temple at Jerusalem. Imagine Zechariah after his encounter with the angel Gabriel: mute, because he had not believed the herald, his heart and eyes bursting with hope…but mute! How would he have communicated with his wife this joyous news? In any event, it appears that sometime after his return, John the Baptist was conceived to this aging couple—a miracle like that experienced by the father and mother of Israel, Abraham and Sarah, in the ancient story.

Why had God chosen Elisabeth, of all people, to bear and raise the prophet announcing the Messiah's coming? She must have been a faith-filled woman who had never given up her faith in the God of Israel as her personal God, regardless of the disappointment that accompanied her empty home. God saw in her an open and willing vessel, one that he filled with the Holy Spirit and prophesied the coming of the Christ when Mary set foot across her doorstep in the sixth month of Elisabeth's pregnancy.

Elisabeth was obviously a person of inner fortitude. She had the strength of character not to forsake God during her barren years as she longed for children. She echoed Job, "the Lord gives and the Lord takes away, blessed be the name of the Lord." God foreknew that Elisabeth's faith and character would positively influence at least two important people. The first was Mary the mother of Christ, who arrived at the beginning of Elisabeth's third trimester and stayed for three months.

The obvious implication is that Mary stayed with Elisabeth at least through the birth of John. We do not know the nature of the interaction between youthful Mary and mature Elisabeth. Certainly, an adolescent Mary may have been a help to older Elisabeth in the final stages of pregnancy. Similarly, Elisabeth may have been a comforting presence to a naïve maiden overwhelmed with a divine pregnancy. Perhaps Mary experienced moments of anxiety, either about her reputation, or more likely, the good name of her betrothed. Maybe Mary was suffering with intense morning sickness and was soothed by Elisabeth's household. We will never know exactly how events transpired, but we can be certain that the example of Elisabeth was a powerful role model for her young cousin.

The other primary benefactor of Elisabeth's wisdom and influence was the baby, infant, toddler, boy, youth, and ultimately man who became John the Baptist. Elisabeth would have handled the domestic duties of raising a Nazirite son without cutting his hair and keeping alcoholic beverages out of the household. Like any mother it is probably true that much of John's essential character shaped under her careful guidance. She succeeded—her son matured into a man of robust faith like his mother, in contrast to the doubt that characterized his father.

And Jesus himself? The Gospels tell us very little about Jesus' childhood, but Elisabeth may have been a favorite aunt and her home may well have been a place that Mary and Joseph took their young family to visit. If so, Jesus would have heard time and again the story of the double miracle births, the audacity of his uncle to disbelieve an angel, the harrowing escape to Egypt, and the details of his and John's births. At the center of it all was Elisabeth: faithful, strong, and righteous.

In short, God saw in Elisabeth something different from what her neighbors saw: strength, courage, faith, security in God's will. God chose Elisabeth to influence the unfolding Christmas story in a powerful way—with a mother's faith and an aunt's love. And it reminds us, during the holidays and throughout the year, that we too have a sphere of influence within which we can share our faith in God's goodness and guidance.

Chapter 5

Herod the Great

After Jesus was born in Bethlehem in Judea, during the time of King Herod, Magi from the east came to Jerusalem and asked, "Where is the one who has been born king of the Jews? We saw his star in the east and have come to worship him. When King Herod heard this he was disturbed, and all Jerusalem with him. When he had called together all the people, chief priests, and teachers of the law, he asked them where the Christ was to be born. "In Bethlehem in Judea," they replied, "for this is what the prophet has written: 'But you, Bethlehem, in the land of Judah, are by no means least among the rulers of Judah; for out of you will come a ruler who will be the shepherd of my people Israel.'" Then Herod called the Magi secretly and found out from them the exact time the star had appeared. He sent them to Bethlehem and said, "Go and make a careful search for the child. As soon as you find him, report to me, so that I too may go and worship him…" [Herod] was furious, and he gave orders to kill all the boys in Bethlehem and its vicinity who were two years old and under, in accordance with the time he had learned from the Magi. Then what was said through the prophet Jeremiah was fulfilled: "A voice is heard in Ramah, weeping and great mourning, Rachel weeping for her children and refusing to be comforted because they are no more." Matthew 2:1-9, 16-19

Herod I (the Great) was the Roman-appointed king over Judea and its environs. In actuality, he was not a Jew and certainly was no heir to David's throne. Ironically, he was Idumean—an Edomite—a descendant of Esau, Israel's cousins, a people neighboring Judea to the east who had spent much of their history in vassalage to Israel's kings. Interestingly, throughout the

Bible the descendants of Esau are characterized as spiritually cold: unreligious, pragmatic, and worldly. Their scion had sold his birthright for immediate gratification offered by a bowl of stew after a long day on the hunt. Esau seemed to never understand that the birthright as well as a subsequent blessing from his father Isaac were not simply about material inheritance but were pregnant with spiritual significance. Moreover, in his anger Esau immediately turns to violence, intending to murder his brother and thus causing Jacob to flee his home. This murderous anger resurfaces in Jewish legend when Esau murders Nimrod, the great hunter and founder of Babel.

This violence marks Esau's descendants in the extra-Biblical Jewish literature. In the Bible, we lose sight of Esau's descendants for centuries except as a rough people living in the wilderness of Mt Seir, but one surfaces in King Saul's attempts to assassinate David. The royal shepherd, Doeg the Edomite, is the only individual in the king's party willing to obey Saul's command to slaughter over 80 members of the priestly family of Ahimelech. Again, the sin of Esau is apparent in his descendant—the willingness to act bold for immediate advancement without regard for spiritual consequences.

Centuries later, another son of Esau—Herod—had established himself as King of Judea, within the Roman system. His accession was not easy, and over time it resulted in marriages for political convenience and numerous murders of political rivals, including his father-in-law, brother, wife, and sons. Herod originally sided with Antony in Rome's civil war, but following Antony's defeat Herod shrewdly and courageously traveled to Rome, using flattery, cunning, and gifts to successfully persuade Antony's rival Octavian (Augustus) to reaffirm Herod's kingship in Judea.

To be successful in Judea meant that Herod had to play a delicate balancing act, demonstrating fealty to imperial Rome while keeping the peace among the non-conforming Jewish population with its religious controversies and foment. Herod's Idumean pragmatism was consonant with the pragmatism of the Roman Empire: he introduced a strategy of imposed order, massive public works, and religious tolerance. The crowning jewel of his public works campaign was to rebuild the Jewish temple, which had been significantly damaged in military campaigns by Pompey (A.D. 63), Crassus (A.D. 54), and Herod himself when first appointed by the Roman Senate. In fact, later in Jesus' life he and his disciples recognize the physical beauty of this very temple, and it is therein that Jesus denounces the materialistic character of the political and religious order of the day.

This is the Herod of Christ's birth: a shrewd political survivor intent on setting up an enduring political dynasty. Like his ancestors he was unconcerned with spiritual things and was cunning, materialistic, and prone to violence. Consequently, when a group of philosopher-kings from the East arrive, perhaps with an extensive baggage train of servants, family members, camels, and gifts, Herod was troubled by their tidings. Moreover, Matthew records that all of Jerusalem "was troubled with him." Why was this so? There are any number of reasons why Jerusalem might have been "troubled," the most logical being that Herod was notorious for seizing the flimsiest pretext as an excuse for executing his real or perceived enemies.

When the Magi arrived, Herod immediately called in the Jewish religious leaders who quickly gave him a verdict: if there was a new king in the offing, he must come from the ancestral seat of King David's family at Bethlehem. Apparently Herod dismissed the religious elite and then hatched a clever plan. He slipped out of the palace clandestinely and asking the Magi to bring him tidings of their search. Imagine the setting: the king arriving in disguise at the Magi's encampment outside the city walls in the dead of night. Or perhaps they were lodged at a fine inn within the city and a masked Herod arrived at midnight unannounced. In any event, he asked them to bring him tidings of the consummation of their search. We can only speculate how he approached them with this missive and whether they were duped by his apparent sincerity. Perhaps he suggested that he would protect the child from the idolatrous Romans or from the frenzies of Jewish religious life.

Of course, the Magi may have seen through his duplicity and recognized the threat Herod posed to the Christ child. However, Herod was charismatic and crafty and may have persuaded them of his pure motives—this is the same Herod who charmed Antony and Cleopatra first and later their arch-enemy Octavian. In any event, the Magi apparently did slip away at night to find the Christ child, perhaps by leaving their retinue on the outskirts of Jerusalem and traveling the short five miles to Bethlehem unaccompanied. We know that they did so at night because they continued to follow their trusty guide—a supernatural star.

When warned by God not to aid Herod, the Magi quietly left the country by another route, and an incensed Herod carried out the second stage of his plan—the ruthless extermination of all male newborns, infants, and toddlers in Bethlehem and its environs. As Bethlehem was probably merely a town of several hundred inhabitants, this meant killing a couple of dozen male babies. Consequently, Herod probably slept content that he had taken every action to preserve his throne.

Herod's descendants likewise bump in and out of the Christian story as power-hungry, self-interested, and unspiritual. For example it is Herod I's son who boasts at a party that he will give his stepdaughter, following a lascivious dance, whatever she wants. She asked for, and received, John the Baptist's head on a platter. That same son, Herod II, wanted to see Jesus perform magic, and disappointed, signals his subservience to Rome by mocking Jesus and placing him under Pontius Pilate's authority for crucifixion. Herod II reveled in the people calling him divine, and died a supernatural death for it. Herod the Great's children and grandchildren persecute the early Church, and it is his great-grandson, Herod Agrippa II, who remarks that he is "almost persuaded" by St. Paul to become a Christian. The clear implication is that Herod Agrippa's reservations are related to his material comfort and status.

Herod and his descendants follow in Esau's footsteps—they failed to appreciate that they were given an opportunity for political stewardship that had moral implications. Instead, they were spiritually deadened and totally focused on personal gratification and power. As children of Esau they were never aware of the spiritual significance of the supernatural drama unfolding around them. Herod's materialism, pragmatism, and spiritual lethargy were in direct contrast to the kind of king that Jesus was coming to be: Wonderful Counselor, the Mighty God, the Everlasting Father, the Prince of Peace. Of course, it is easy to be spiritually dormant in the frenetic race of materialistic twenty-first century culture. Nonetheless, the choice is ours whether or not to open our eyes to our spiritual and moral responsibilities in the sphere of influence that God has given us.

Chapter 6

Jesus the Servant

Here is my servant, whom I uphold, my chosen one in whom I delight.
I will put my Spirit on him and he will bring justice to the nations.
He will not shout or cry out, or raise his voice in the streets.
A bruised reed he will not break, and a smoldering wick he will not snuff out.
In faithfulness he will bring forth justice;
He will not falter or be discouraged until he establishes justice on earth.
Isaiah 42:1-4

The people of Jesus' day anticipated a warrior Messiah. In part, this was due to a popular apocalyptic literature that developed in the period which focused heavily on the coming Christ as a political-military figure who would restore the glory of David's kingdom via battlefield triumphs. The average Jew expected that someday the Messiah would charge in on a white horse followed by the hosts of heaven and slay Israel's enemies, establishing an eternal kingdom. The apocalyptic genre could be fantastic at times, but more often it was rooted in key scriptural passages associated with prophets such as Daniel, Ezekiel, and Isaiah. There is an obvious parallel in our day with the various "end times" novels written by evangelical Christian authors who compose fiction around their careful study and elaboration of apocalyptic events, as they understand them, taken from the Book of Revelation and the Old Testament prophets.

One scriptural basis for such views originated in texts from Isaiah, Israel's greatest prophet after Moses. Isaiah describes a millennial Messiah who will ultimately establish an earthly kingdom. A theme permeating Isaiah 42, as well as other chapters (i.e. Isaiah chapters 9 and 32), is the establishment of peace, security, and justice, especially for the poor. Jews of Christ's day could easily associate with this because they were peasants within the greatest empire the world has ever seen, and they faced constant scrutiny and often outright persecution for their peculiar beliefs and uncooperativeness, resulting in the destruction of the Israel and its temple in A.D. 70.

However, the Jews did not know how to handle accompanying images of a servant Messiah, a suffering Christ. At the advent of his ministry Christ directly quotes from Isaiah 61 in order to reveal his identity.[4] Shortly after Jesus began to minister, he returned to his hometown synagogue in the village of Nazareth. Everyone knew him intimately. The old men nodded their heads as he began to speak, they had known him to be "a good boy" since he was a child. The younger men remembered growing up alongside Jesus, playing games and swimming in the river. When Jesus opened the Torah and began to speak that day, his neighbors marveled in pride that the local boy appeared to have the makings of a real prophet, just like his cousin John the Baptist. However, moments later he told them that this Messianic prophecy, the one from Isaiah 61 which they could all quote from by heart, referred to *him*. In shock at the blasphemy, they dragged him out of the synagogue and nearly threw him off a cliff to die. Here is what he read to them:

> "The Spirit of the Sovereign Lord is on me, because the Lord has anointed me to preach good news to the poor. He has sent me to bind up the brokenhearted, to proclaim freedom for the captives and release from darkness for the prisoners, to proclaim the year of the Lord's favor…"

---

[4] Luke 4:18-19.

Jesus revealed his Messiah-ship by focusing carefully on his mission to redeem hearts, heal lives, restore hope, and nurture faith rather than lead an army and defend an earthly kingdom. He directed his mission to those in society who needed him most: the dispossessed, the marginalized, and the impoverished. A refrain throughout the Gospels is that even when Jesus was exhausted, he was "moved with compassion" by the masses because he perceived them as "sheep without a shepherd."

During his earthly ministry he was attempting a far more difficult battle than that for territory or plunder: he was trying to conquer the treacherous kingdom of the human heart, redeem it from sin, and turn people toward one another as God's agents of service and charity. Certainly Christ did not relinquish his claim to a tangible throne, but throughout his ministry he declared that he would return to establish that kingdom.

During the holiday season, we should recognize two great truths from these pre-Christmas, prophetic passages. The first is that Jesus was the Christ for everyone—the prophecy proclaims that he comes to save, heal, and give purpose to the lives of common people. Indeed, the conception of Christ took place in the womb of an unknown maiden betrothed to a common carpenter in a modest village on the edge of civilization, and was initially attended by animals and uncouth sheepherders. This was to become the pattern of Christ's ministry: seeking out those who needed him most such as lepers, prostitutes, tax collectors, and even Gentiles.

Second, if God's example was deep concern for the lost and needy, then at all times, but especially during the celebration of Jesus' birth, we should be so concerned as well. Jesus initiated his ministry by calling attention to the Messiah's role as healer and comforter. Decades later, he concluded his earthly ministry after the resurrection by charging his disciples to preach the good news to all people everywhere and to unleash healing and restoration in his name. This is the charge for the Church today: to preach the gospel, bring healing, proclaim liberty, and proclaim that today is the day of salvation.

Chapter 7

The Unexpected Christ

Nevertheless, there will be no more gloom for those who were in distress. In the past he humbled the land of Zebulun and the land of Naphtali, but in the future he will honor Galilee of the Gentiles, by the way of the sea, along the Jordan—

> *The people walking in darkness have seen a great light;*
> *On those living in the land of the shadow of death a light has dawned.*
> *You have enlarged the nation and increased their joy;*
> *They rejoice before you as people rejoice at the harvest,*
> *As men rejoice when dividing the plunder.*
> *For as in the day of Midian's defeat,*
> *you have shattered the yoke that burdens them,*
> *the bar across their shoulders, the rod of their oppressor.*
> *Every warrior's boot used in battle and every garment rolled in blood will be destined for burning,*
> *Will be fuel for the fire.*
> *For to us a child is born,*
> *To us a son is given,*
> *And the government will be on his shoulders.*
> *And he will be called Wonderful, Counselor, Mighty God,*
> *Everlasting Father, Prince of Peace.*
> *Of the increase of his government and peace there will be no end.*
> *He will reign on David's throne and over his kingdom,*
> *Establishing and upholding it with justice and righteousness*
> *From that time on forever.*

The zeal of the Lord Almighty will accomplish this.
Isaiah 9:1-7

This famous passage is indelibly imprinted on the mind and in the ears of anyone who has heard George Frederick Handel's *Messiah*:

> Wonderful!
> Counselor!
> The Mighty God!
> The Everlasting Father!
> The Prince…of…Peace!

To the contemporary Christian looking back on Christmas, with two thousand years of theological hindsight, the passage from Isaiah obviously refers to *two* comings of the Messiah. He did come and bring a "great light" to people "walking in darkness." He did shatter the burdens oppressing many: disease, heartbreak, alienation from God, and spiritual distress. Christian theology suggests that Christ will return and fulfill the rest of the prophecy by establishing a kingdom and "upholding it with justice and righteousness from that time on and forever." In this, the world has a blessed hope for the future.

However, this passage must have been in the minds of those who knew and observed Jesus of Galilee in the first century A.D. Undoubtedly it caused confusion for many. They were living under the rule of the Roman Empire and lacked political and social freedom, which would culminate a generation after Christ's death with the destruction of the temple and the deportation of those Jews not slaughtered in a futile insurrection against Rome. The people were experiencing a spiritual darkness as well—a silent era four centuries long in which no prophet spoke directly on behalf of God until the coming of John the Baptist.

The passage apparently describes rejoicing at a Jewish renaissance and utilizes images of battle and defeating long-standing foes, suggestive of political and military might. The carpenter from Nazareth obviously did not fit the bill; in fact, his actions supported the status quo. He did not command the centurions and tax collectors to leave Roman service, but rather to serve in a righteous manner. He paid his taxes. Worse, he was entertained by tax collectors. He turned his wit and irony on his own people's religious establishment and uttered not a word of direct reproach against the Romans. Moreover, he avoided the centers of Jewish power as well as the ruling (the Herodians) and religious (Pharisees, Sadducees) elite, instead seeking out the poor.

On closer examination, however, this passage does ring true as evidence of Jesus' ministry. First, he did bring *light*. He brought an illuminated understanding of the Scripture and of God's love for humanity. Indeed, many marveled at his teaching, for he "taught with the authority" of the Godhead (Mark 1:14) rather than the quibbling and proverbs of Jewish rabbis. Moreover, the light provided clarity regarding God's plan for salvation and desire for personal intimacy rather than rote ritual. Finally, Jesus provided an example that people could see about how God could bring a spiritual dawn to those walking in the valley of the shadow of death.

We intellectually know that for those to whom Jesus ministered—those that he healed, delivered, or ministered to, "in the shadow of death a light...dawned." In other words, he also brought *joy*: the joy of deliverance, of wholeness, of mercy. Imagine the spiritual wonder of an individual apprehending the Savior as Christ heals a deformed limb, casts out a demon, or forgives a sinful heart. Consider how you or I would feel if Christ healed our crippled legs, dramatically released us from alcohol addiction, or brought our prodigal child home. For many of us who have witnessed and experienced the light of Christ, we should be reflecting our joy and thanksgiving.

But that is not what happened to the Babe of Bethlehem. The Christmas child, who brought joy and light to a dark and lost world, was the Light of the World. But even those who were healed miraculously and his closest disciples forsake him just a short time later, making them complicit in his murder at Calvary.

Thus, this prophecy from Isaiah had to be confusing in Jesus' day. The people expected a Messiah who would invert the socio-political order of the time and return them to the top, as masters once again of David's kingdom, living in a golden age of peace and prosperity. Christ did come, but he spent his time preaching repentance among the poor and lowly. Christ did bring light to those in darkness, relieving the terrible burden carried by some, establishing peace in the hearts of those who believed. But to others he was an enigma, a phenomenon that both exceeded and fell far short of their expectations for a Savior. Today, we too are confronted by Jesus the Man and Jesus the Son of God: how will we respond to the enigma of God's Son accepting weakness and death that we might be spiritually transformed in the midst of an imperfect and fallen world? Will we reject him as not meeting our notion of a Messiah, or accept God's unexpected Savior and surrender to His will and to His way?

Chapter 8

Shepherds Keeping Watch

And there were shepherds living out in the fields nearby, keeping watch over their flocks at night. An angel of the Lord appeared to them, and the glory of the Lord shone around them, and they were terrified. "Do not be afraid. I bring you good news of great joy that will be for all the people. Today in the town of David a Savior has been born to you; he is Christ the Lord. This will be a sign to you: you will find a baby wrapped in cloths and lying in a manger." Suddenly a great company of the heavenly host appeared with the angel, praising God and saying, "Glory to God in the highest, and on earth peace to men on whom his favor rests." When the angels had left them and gone into heaven, the shepherds said to one another, "Let's go to Bethlehem and see this thing that has happened, which the Lord has told us about. So they hurried off and found Mary and Joseph and the baby who was lying in the manger. When they had seen him, they spread the word concerning what had been told them about this child, and all who heard it were amazed at what the shepherds said to them…The shepherds returned, glorifying and praising God for all the things they had heard and seen, which were just as they had been told. Luke 2: 8-18, 20

One wonders, "Why did God choose to direct his angelic heralds to this particular group of shepherds? What makes them so special? On the one hand, probably not very much. Sheepherding is not generally considered to be a distinguished profession. On the other hand, there was something about this motley band that made God trust sending an angelic message to them. So, what was special about these shepherds?

Shepherding can be quiet work on a mild day with no predators about. But shepherds must remain vigilant, particularly at night, lest an inquisitive lamb stray or a predator insinuate itself into the flock's margins. Shepherding can mean long hours of outdoor solitary confinement, battered by elements, and awareness of the temper of the sheep which can sometimes alert the shepherd when danger is approaching. However, most of the time the sheep are blissfully unaware of impending crisis and it is up to the shepherd alone to spot the danger lurking on the edge of the flock.

When the angels accosted the shepherds, most of Bethlehem's inhabitants were sound asleep in their beds. Had the angels appeared over a district of the city, it is likely that the population within would have slept through the announcement of the coming Messiah. Imagine, the heavenly host singing above the empty streets of slumbering Bethlehem…

More importantly than being physically awake, it is apparent that these shepherds were also spiritually aware. They were chosen because they would know how to respond to the message. Thus, they are an example of the "good ground" Jesus spoke of in the Parable of the Sower. Recall that in the parable, the same redemptive message, symbolized by seed, is proffered to numerous hearers, but that in each case it is received differently. Some hearers ignored the call, others embraced it temporarily, and some seed was accepted, took root, and grew robustly.

Such a scenario may have occurred that night in the hills surrounding Bethlehem. Certainly there were other shepherds in the vicinity. For all we know, those other shepherds may have heard the angels' song, but their encounter is lost to history because they chose not to act. Shepherds on the north side of Bethlehem, for instance, might have hearts and minds that were "stony ground:" they refused to listen, clamping their hands over their ears and shutting their eyes, either out of fear for their own safety or due to bitterness, perhaps occasioned by personal loss, toward spiritual matters. Unfortunately it is not uncommon for people to acknowledge God's existence, but turn their back on him deliberately.

Perhaps another couple of shepherds, those on the west side, heard the message and saw the angels while on duty, and tried to wake their sleeping comrades. These were enthusiastic, at least initially. But, when their sleepy fellow shepherds finally awoke, the angels were gone and those who witnessed the heavenly choir were convinced by the complaints and ridicule of those they had just woken that the experience was a dream. They were like seeds that quickly sprang up into plants, but withered in the sun. Their experience was temporary and had no depth.

A third set of shepherds, maybe grazing on the south side of Bethlehem, eagerly responded at first to the message, but after a few energetic steps toward Bethlehem, doubts arose. Their thoughts quickly changed from, "Wow, a miracle sent to us!" to "Boy, it's a long way to walk at night...what about the sheep...did the angel say "in a manger"...that doesn't sound like a king to me....this is too much trouble...besides, who will watch over the sheep?" They gave up before they ever got close. The truth in their heart was choked by the weeds of doubt.

One way or the other, God did present the message to a group of shepherds whose hearts were good soil, and upon hearing the message, they acted in faith and sought the newborn Messiah. Imagine, a band of shepherds trolling the streets of the village of Bethlehem, looking for mangers where a baby might be asleep in the middle of the night. Finally they found an exhausted new mother, an anxious father, a tiny newborn baby lying in a feeding trough...and the shepherds worshipped, giving thanks to God for the miracle they were experiencing.

The experience changed them. Instead of hurrying back to the flock, they spread the word about what they had seen and what the angel had told them. They shared the good news of a Messiah's birth with others, representing a harvest "a hundred times more than was sown." The shepherds were spiritually aware and grasped the promise of God, providing an example of active faith and witnessing about their experience.

Likewise, God's message of love and purpose is knocking on hearts today. For some it is the initial call to life change, for others it is a directive to share the truth that resides in their heart. In either case, be like the shepherds who assisted the harvest, not like those who missed the opportunity to participate in God's redemptive plan.

Chapter 9

What's in a Name?

[an angel appeared to Joseph]... "you are to give him the name Jesus, because he will save his people from their sins." Matthew 1:21

[God sent the angel Gabriel to Mary] "...you will be with child and give birth to a son, and you are to give him the name Jesus..." Luke 1:31

In both accounts of Jesus' birth, an angel tells each of his parents separately and distinctly that the child is to be named "Jesus." The name is the Greek form of "Joshua," a common name among Jews throughout history and likely popular in the first century A.D., but a surprisingly uncommon one in Jesus' lineage. We know this because Matthew and Luke record the genealogies of Joseph and Mary's families (respectively) and there is only a single Joshua named in Jesus' ancestors over the centuries.

Today parents generally choose a name for their child based on personal preferences, fads, or the historic meaning of a name, regardless of familial or ethnic associations. Such was not the case among Jews of Mary and Joseph's generation, where names promulgated rich family associations. Moreover, naming—to give a name to, to give meaning to—a child was symbolic and even mystical in that a name could be tied prophetically to the character, personality, and even destiny of that new person. In short, by calling him "Jesus" Mary and Joseph were affirming and witnessing to their faith in the unique birth and spiritual significance of this child.

Importantly, it was God who chose the name of this baby, and it was God who sent the angel Gabriel to each parent to instruct them of His choice. It was a name with two powerful associations in Jewish history: a priest and a leader. The former we know little about, he was Joshua the High Priest who led the people of God in worship at the end of the second captivity.[5]

It should be obvious that the second historical link—to Moses' lieutenant—as well as the meaning of the name itself are both important here. Joshua, son of Nun, was originally named "Hosea," which means "salvation." It is probable that his parents, groaning as slaves with their friends and relatives under the lash of Pharaoh in Egypt, named their son "salvation" as a desperate prayer, "God, please…we beg of you…save us! Save our baby son, that he might not endure the terrible bondage of your people Israel."

When Hosea was a man, God answered their prayer. God delivered the people of Israel from physical slavery as well as removed them from the idolatry of Egypt and gave them a unique and holy spiritual relationship with him. Thus, Moses changed the name of his favorite subordinate, Hosea, to Joshua (or Je-Hosea) which means "God is salvation."[6] This change of name was symbolic and testified to the marvelous power of God that brought the plagues on Egypt, released the Israelites, carried them across the Red Sea, sustained them in the wilderness for forty years, and ultimately was to give them the Promised Land as an inheritance.

It was Joshua who shadowed the steps of Moses the lawgiver, Israel's greatest prophet. Joshua was the only person to follow Moses onto Mount Sinai when the Ten Commandments were given. It was Joshua who stayed in the tabernacle worshipping the Lord when Moses had to leave to attend his duties. Joshua was one of the two spies who brought back a good report about

---

[5] Zechariah 6:11, 12.
[6] Numbers 13:6.

Canaan, urging the people to take possession of God's salvation and promises. And in the end it was Joshua, not Moses, who actually led the people of Israel into the Promised Land.

Joshua led the Israelites in victory after victory, not by the raw might of his sword, but by the direction of God. It is important to recognize that Joshua's greatest triumphs, as well as defeats, were spiritual in nature—his life example was "God is salvation." It took divine intervention for Joshua to defeat the Amalekites in battle and later for him to lead Israel across the raging Jordan River on dry ground in a scene reminiscent of deliverance a generation earlier at the Red Sea. It was God's divine power that brought down the walls of Jericho, and it was when Joshua was not clearly following God's will that Israel experienced setbacks at Ai and in the matter of the Gibeonites.

By naming this new baby, the Messiah, "Jesus," God was explicitly telling the world that salvation was through God alone, not through religious observance as the Pharisees believed nor through the political power of the Herodians. This new Joshua was to bring a spiritual salvation to his people as did the Joshua of old. The angel affirmed, "he will save his people *from* their sins," not "he will save his people in their sins" or "despite their sins." This Joshua was not to be simply a general, politician, or earthly king—he was to bring spiritual light and life to the people of Israel. He would initiate a new kingdom, a new Promised Land.

Of course, this baby would grow into a boy, a teenager, and eventually mature into a man thirty years of age before beginning his public ministry. We know little about what happened in his life during this time, and how this Jesus came to awareness that he was the Christ. We do know, however, that just prior to his ministry he spent forty days and forty nights in fasting and prayer, ultimately being tempted by Satan to forsake his spiritual calling and accept an earthly kingdom. When Jesus had successfully passed this time of testing and just before he begins his ministry, the Scripture says that angels came and ministered unto him. Perhaps the message that the angels brought was the same that an angel gave to the Old Testament Joshua when he took over as leader of Israel, a message that is true for all who accept that in Jesus Christ "God is salvation:"

> "I will never leave you nor forsake you...Be strong and very courageous. Be careful to obey all the law my servant Moses gave you; do not turn from it to the right or to the left, that you may be successful wherever you go. Do not let this Book of the Law depart from your mouth, meditate on it day and night so that you may be careful to do everything written in it. Then you will be prosperous and successful. Have I not commanded you? Be strong and courageous. Do not be terrified, do not be discouraged, for the Lord your God will be with you wherever you go."[7]

---

[7] Joshua 1:5-9.

Chapter 10

Jesus of Biloxi

When they [the Magi] had gone, an angel of the Lord appeared to Joseph in a dream. "Get up," he said, "take the child and his mother and escape to Egypt. Stay there until I tell you, for Herod is going to search for the child to kill him." So he got up, took the child and his mother during the night and left for Egypt where he stayed until the death of Herod…After Herod died, an angel of the Lord appeared in a dream to Joseph in Egypt and said, "Get up, take the child and his mother and go to the land of Israel, for those who were trying to take the child's life are dead." So he got up, took the child and his mother, and went to the land of Israel. But when he heard that Archelaus was reigning in Judea in place of his father Herod, he was afraid to go there. Having been warned in a dream, he withdrew too the district of Galilee and he went and lived in a town called Nazareth. So was fulfilled what was said through the prophets: "He will be called a Nazarene." Matthew 2:13-15, 19-23

Jesus was brought to the town of Nazareth at an early age and would spend most of his life in its environs. Nazareth could truly be called the family home because it was Mary's home prior to the events surrounding Jesus' birth. It was in Nazareth that the angel Gabriel announced that she would bear the Messiah, and it is possible that Nazareth was Joseph's original home as well. Nazareth was a rural community in the region of Galilee, far from the political and social center of the Jewish people in the capital of Jerusalem in the province of Judea. In fact, when Jews from Galilee decided to make the journey to Jerusalem, they often traveled around the intermediate province of

Samaria in order to shun the people and syncretistic religion practiced there. Consequently, Jesus' childhood and much of his adult life were spent in a tiny village marked by parochial obligations and concerns, but certainly characterized by regional and national obscurity.

"Jesus" was a common name for Jewish boys in the first century because it was the Greek form of "Joshua," the great Hebrew leader who led Israel in conquering the Promised Land. Undoubtedly many parents named their children "Jesus" as a sort of faith statement that God would eventually save his people from Roman oppression. In this context, we can be certain that the appellation "Jesus of Nazareth," as unique in his day as "Jesus of Biloxi" would be today, meant that Jesus would not be confused with all of the other men named Jesus when his ministry led him to major population centers.

Hence, Jesus originating from Nazareth was noteworthy in at least three ways. The first is that some commentators believe that there is a pun or word association between "Nazareth" and the calling of the "Nazirite." The Old Testament law specified a peculiar type of consecrated person set apart for special ministry who was required to live a modest lifestyle that included abstinence from wine and strict observance of Jewish dietary laws. Samson, Samuel, and later John the Baptist—all born supernaturally to parents without children and divinely ordained as prophets—were examples of Nazirites. Although Jesus was not called to live the asceticism of the Nazirite order, his birth was supernaturally inspired and he was divinely appointed to live in special relationship with God.

Other commentators have observed a second word association between "Nazareth" and "netzar," the Hebrew word for "branch." The idea is that Jesus of Nazareth is the Branch, a strong and fruitful limb that grows from the Davidic line and is rooted in God's earliest promises to Israel to make the Jews prosperous and fruitful. Centuries before Jesus' birth Isaiah wrote,

> A shoot will come up from the stump of Jesse; from his roots a Branch will bear fruit. The Spirit of the Lord will rest on him; the Spirit of wisdom and of understanding; the Sprit of counsel and of power; the Spirit of knowledge and of the fear of the Lord, and he will delight in the fear of the Lord.[8]

The third and most obvious association of "Nazareth" is the irony that the Messiah would hail from such an obscure location. In modern terms, it would be like saying "Jesus of Biloxi" or "Jesus of Gallup." Indeed, the Bible suggests that there may have been a derogatory aphorism regarding Nazareth in Jesus' day: "Can anything good come out of Nazareth?"[9]

Throughout his ministry, Jesus' Nazarene roots made him an object of ridicule, a rube, a rustic, or perhaps a "red-neck." He is called "Jesus the Nazarene" or "Jesus of Nazareth" by the crowds observing his miracles and the religious leaders of his day. The Nazarene identity is so strong that the mere association indicts Peter on the night of Jesus' capture. When Peter denied Christ, he was first accused of "being with *that* Nazarene," second of being "one of Them," and finally derided as "a Galilean." It is likely that Peter had a bad haircut, rough clothing, and a provincial accent all of which contributed to marking Jesus and his followers as "hicks from the sticks." Years later even the apostle Paul, certainly among the most erudite of the early Church, was identified by the religious elite as a leader of the "Nazarene sect" (read "Biloxi sect") when he was accused before the Roman governor Felix.

---

[8] Isaiah 11:1-3.
[9] John 1:45.

The prophets had warned that the Messiah would be common and even despised. Isaiah wrote that the Christ would "have no beauty or majesty to attract us to him" and would be "despised and rejected of men." The Psalm that Jesus quotes from when expiring on the cross, "My God, my God, why have you forsaken me?" goes on to prophesy, "I am a worm...scorned by men and despised by the people." Similarly, the passage that Matthew cites when Jesus cleared the Temple of moneychangers ("zeal for your house consumes me") says of the Christ, "I endure scorn for your sake, and shame covers my face. I am a stranger to my brothers, an alien..."[10]

In short, "Jesus of Nazareth" was a nobody from nowhere, born to obscure parents with a certain mystery hanging over his birth. He and his associates lived on the margins of society and were represented as bumpkins to the elite of the day. Moreover, Jesus spent his ministry breaking every possible social taboo: touching lepers, dining with tax collectors, protecting adulteresses. Why did God go to so much trouble to put Jesus in the backwater?

Jesus' ministry was to bring hope and deliverance to a people in need. Isaiah prophesied that "the people long in darkness have seen a great light."[11] That light, growing stronger during the three years of his ministry, began to shine in the darkness of the Jewish political and social wilderness, ultimately growing to eclipse all other religious movements in history. More importantly, it seems that whereas some people were fixated on where Jesus grew up, that God was demanding that they put aside their simplistic prejudices and look at the man himself.

Jesus demonstrated time and again that he was the fulfillment of prophecy, that his teaching was centered in the Old Testament, and that his miracles gave witness to the omnipotence of Jehovah God. This was evidence demanding a verdict, not to

---

[10] These verses are found at Isaiah 53:2-3; Psalm 22:6; Psalm 69:7, 8 respectively.
[11] Psalm 22:6.

be confused with who Jesus knew, was related to, or what he was wearing. God was demanding, through the peculiarities of Jesus' background and associations that people look at his message and actions and consider whether or not he was the Messiah sent to save them from their sins. Unfortunately, in Jesus day the people failed to see past his rustic roots. Even on his triumphal entry into Jerusalem, when asked who is arriving, the people failed to say "Jesus the Messiah," instead answering, "Here he comes, Jesus the Nazarene." Today we are confronted with the same opportunity: to consider the facts and make a decision—was he simply Jesus from Nazareth (Biloxi), or is he the Son of God and worthy of our adoration?

Chapter 11

The Light of the World

In the beginning was the word, and the Word was with God, and the Word was God. He was with God in the beginning. Through him all things were made; without him nothing was made that was made. In him was life, and that life was the light of men. The light shines in the darkness, but the darkness has not understood it. There came a man who was sent from God his name was John. He came as a witness to testify concerning that light, so that through him all men might believe. He himself was not the light; he came only as a witness to the light. The true light that gives light to every man was coming into the world. He was in the world, and though the world was made through him, the world did not recognize him. He came to that which was his own, but his own did not receive him. Yet to all who received him, to those who believed in his name, he gave the right to become children of God—children born not of natural descent, nor of human decision or a husband's will, but born of God. The Word became flesh and made his dwelling among us. We have seen his glory, the glory of the One and Only, who came from the Father, full of grace and truth.
John 1:1-14

"In the beginning was the Word..." Only Matthew and Luke tell the Christmas story in detail. Mark's Gospel opens with the advent of Christ's adult ministry—with Jesus' baptism by John the Baptist. Scholars believe that the distinctive approaches are due to different intended audiences. Mark was written shortly after Jesus' death as a brief, immediate record of events. Matthew was designed to persuade Jewish readers that Christ fulfilled the Old Testament Messianic requirements, whereas Luke was directed to a Gentile audience.

The book of John is believed to have been written somewhat later and complements the other gospels with unique contributions, such as this rich poetic imagery. Scholars and readers tend to focus on the lovely literary style of the opening verses or on the Christological claims regarding the person of Jesus—that he is one with the Father from the beginning and is responsible for the entire created order.

However, it is the imagery of light which is most striking as it parallels much in the Christmas story. Light promotes wholeness in at least two ways—it provides the ability to see as well as warmth. "In him was life, and the life was the light of men." Christ was one with the Creator, who had originally spoken, "Let there be light!" Shortly thereafter God spoke again, "let us create man in our own image." Adam became a "living soul" only after God placed a spark of spiritual vitality in him through the breath of God himself. Adam became real-life, different from any other living creature, a sort of Pinocchio-the-real-boy when God breathed life into him. That life is the light of men.

Jesus came to earth as the Christmas Savior to bring light to a dark world. This meant that after the tragedy of the Fall and millennia of sin, God was inaugurating a new beacon, a new lighthouse, to save humanity from destruction. However, it is important to see that John observed the light shining in utter darkness. In fact, John states that the light was misunderstood and not even recognized by many. This image is important because it raises the issue of the Christmas tragedy: although God sent his Son into the world, the environment was so spiritually polluted and confused that humanity did not recognize the life-saving opportunity right in front it. Such opacity may have stemmed from pride, ignorance, a poverty of spiritual depth, or a lack of trust, but regardless, it resulted in the blindness of the earth dwellers. Indeed, the people of Jesus day, and ours, are like drowning swimmers pulling down their would-be saviors or like the inhabitants of Plato's cave, whose entire reality was based on only the faintest shadows of the real world.

Christ brought light. He clearly distinguished between God's love for us and all the hypocrisy and prideful duties associated with conceited religiosity. Christ shone his light into the lives of those who needed him the most, but was available to all, regardless of rank or status. And Christ illuminated the true, loving nature of his heavenly father to a people long-estranged from a caring parent.

Christ also brought warmth. His message was intimacy with God: "to those who believed in his name, he gave the right to become children of God..." His lifestyle was compassion and interest for the well-being of the individual human beings around him. His calling was to provide an in-person demonstration of how much God values his creation, so much so that he was willing to send the light of the world to thaw the bleak environment of human spirituality.

Finally, the symbolism of light is apparent throughout the Nativity narratives as well. Jesus was born in a second-rate town in a desolate corner of the Roman empire. To add insult to injury, he was born ignominiously in a stable or barn, in the middle of the night with only an anxious set of parents and numerous domesticated beasts to attend the birth. Strangely, it was here that a powerful beam flicked on, a radiance that would redeem billions of people over the centuries.

The Christmas story records that momentary opening of heaven and its light bursting forth. The Magi followed a once-in-history star through the night. The angelic host exploded through the Judean wilderness, illuminating the night with "Glory to God." Zechariah, Mary, and Joseph were all dazzled by individual angelic encounters. Nevertheless, in the days following Jesus' birth, the light seemed to immediately fade, as Jesus the infant retracted to the obscurity of a modest carpenter's home and retreated out of Palestine to Egypt. It would be three decades before the light of the world would be revealed for who he was: the sun of history, the North Star of human existence, the center of the universe. And today the choice lies before all of mankind: do we embrace the brilliance of Jesus Christ, or do we close our eyes and painfully bumble our life away on the dark planet?

Chapter 12

The Visitation of the Magi

After Jesus was born in Bethlehem in Judea, during the time of King Herod, Magi from the east came to Jerusalem and asked, "Where is the one who has been born king of the Jews? We saw his star in the east and have come to worship him. When King Herod heard this he was disturbed, and all Jerusalem with him. When he had called together all the people's chief priests and teachers of the law, he asked them where the Christ was to be born. "In Bethlehem in Judea," they replied, "for this is what the prophet has written:

> *'But you, Bethlehem, in the land of Judah, are by no means least among the rulers of Judah; for out of you will come a ruler who will be the shepherd of my people Israel.'"*

Then Herod called the Magi secretly and found out from them the exact time the star had appeared. He sent them to Bethlehem and said, "Go and make a careful search for the child. As soon as you find him, report to me, so that I too may go and worship him." After they had heard the king, they went on their way, and the star they had seen in the east went ahead of them until it stopped over the place where the child was. When they saw the star, they were overjoyed. On coming to the house, they saw the child with his mother Mary, and they bowed down and worshiped him. Then they opened their treasures and presented him with gifts of gold and of incenses and of myrrh. And having been warned in a dream not to go back to Herod, they returned to their country by another route. Matthew 2:1-12

The wise men were princes and sages in their own country, yet they traveled across Mesopotamia and worshipped a babe born in a stable. Little of their story is known to us, but they exemplify faith as defined in Hebrews 11:1: "Faith is the substance of things hoped for, the evidence of things not seen."[12] Their story of resolute faith, travel from the east following a promise, and the consummation of their sojourn is reminiscent of that of another faith-traveler from the east, the progenitor of the Jewish nation: Abraham. Understanding a bit about Abraham's life and mission can help us identify features of the Magi's faith and quest, and aid us in considering the risks and costs associated with their search for Jesus.

Thus, it may help us to understand the magi if we think of them through the frame of Abraham. They were wise men, probably well-versed not only in astronomy and astrology, but in all the sciences and public affairs of their day. They were from the east, perhaps from Chaldea, like Abraham. They "traversed afar" in order to find a Prince who would be a king of a heavenly city, and they risked much in going. They crossed "moor and mountain, field and fountain [and desert]" in search of something much bigger than themselves. This was faith, and the cost of the journey is worthy of our inspection.

The writer of Hebrews identifies Abraham as the paragon of faith, "for he was looking forward to the city with foundations, whose architect and builder is God."[13] However, Abraham originated in the pagan, astrologically-oriented culture to the east of what became Israel (Ur of the Chaldees), perhaps the same general area that the Magi called home a millennium later. In answer to God's call Abraham, and later the Magi, traveled across Mesopotamia, probably via Syria, looking for evidence of

---

[12] This well-known exposition is from the King James Version. The NIV translation is lesser known: "Now faith is being sure of what we hope for and certain of what we do not see."

[13] Hebrews 11:10.

an eternal kingdom. Like Abraham, they were people of some wealth. Indeed, it is likely that the Magi far outstripped Abraham's significant resources, and their education and training reinforced their privileged birthright. Incredibly, a group of these Magi, motivated by some prophetic message in conjunction with an astronomical event endowed with astrological significance, left their home to pilgrimage to the birthplace of a new Jewish king.

We assume that there were three kings because of the number of gifts given, but we do not know for certain. So a group of at least two, and perhaps many more, Magi made it to Jerusalem in the wake of Jesus birth. If they traveled lightly, they may have pushed directly across the direct but dangerous eastern desert caravan route from their home in Babylon, Nineveh, or perhaps even further to the east. However, it is more likely that they traveled with an entourage that included servants and perhaps close family members. In this case they probably traveled in some elegance and in numbers via the lengthier Syrian route, and like Abraham of old, they would have traveled at a much slower pace. Certainly they would have been on their guard because the caravan routes and wilderness areas were lawless and a party of such obvious wealth would be tempting prey for brigands.

We know nothing of their departure from home. Some perhaps believed in their quest and wished them Godspeed, others, likely to include some wives and intimates, may have thought it a fool's quest, and a dangerous one at that. Certainly, Abraham faced such sentiments, for we know that his father and a large company left Ur but never made it past the first leg of the journey west to Haran. Like Abraham, questions and doubts must have been in the Magi's thoughts over the weeks of travel across a large chunk of the Near East. Consider the doubts, desires, and imaginings of the wise men when compelled to think it over, day after day, during the monotony of the march: "Did we read the signs correctly?" "Will we find the king?" "Is there really such a king?"

Their long sojourn brought them to Jerusalem, home of the reigning king of the region, Herod the Great. Naturally they might have assumed that a son had recently been born to Herod's family and thus the Magi were ready to honor the babe. Imagine their surprise at the blank looks on the faces of Herod's courtiers when queried about the new king!

Of course, God's beacon led them ultimately the final six miles to Bethlehem, to a "house" there. If some time had passed since the birth, it is likely that Joseph was working, but doubtless the conditions of Jesus' domestic life were humble. What thought the Magi? That the signs were mistaken? That they had erred? That they had chanced upon a child of poverty rather than a child of power and significance? Abraham probably wondered the same thing when he was attacked by pagan armies, watched the sin of Sodom and Gomorrah envelope his nephew's family, and had to flee the Promised Land due to famine.

In short, like Abraham, the Magi followed God's signs far, and like Abraham they routinely encountered the unexpected. However, their faith was not shallow. When they arrived at the place where baby Jesus and his parents were lodged, they bowed before the child. By doing so they offered respect to this baby born to the humblest of parents. The Magi offered gifts, presents fit for royal personage: priceless gold, fragrant incense, and costly perfume associated with burial. But in addition to the gifts and the ritual bow, they worshipped. The Magi not only bowed before this baby, they praised him as the Son of God and gave glory to God for manifesting himself in the flesh. They humbled themselves, regardless of their wealth, wisdom, status, or position as worshippers, as lower-in-rank, as servants, as unworthy before the Christ child.

In sum, the Magi experienced the vindication of their faith because they believed and acted. Like Abraham, over the months and miles of an exhausting journey they maintained a sense of the big picture, an eternal perspective on the end of their mission. They understood that they were searching for the pearl of great price and they had the wisdom not to be disappointed when their findings differed from their expectations. Moreover, they had the humility to accept, as Abraham did, that God's plan might be far different from their own, and that they were just witnessing the first fruits of a much greater harvest. They were seeking a heavenly city and an eternal plan, whose founder and builder is God.

Thus, during this holiday season, or any season, we must reflect on the quality of our faith journey. Are we willing to take the risks associated with hope? Are we willing to act in faith on the inspiration that God has put before us? Will we persevere in our faith journey, even when we are discouraged or the results are disappointing? Abraham found the Promised Land and these Magi found the Christ, but the vast majority of their friends and associates never even set out—are you going to act or be left behind?

Chapter 13

The Magnificat

Mary said:
> *My soul glorifies the Lord, and my spirit rejoices in God my Savior, for he has been mindful of the humble state of his servant.*
> *From now on all generations will call me blessed, for the Mighty One has done great things for me—*
> *Holy is his name.*
> *His mercy extends to those who fear him, from generation to generation.*
> *He has performed mighty deeds with his arm; he has scattered those who are proud in their inmost thoughts.*
> *He has brought down rulers from their thrones but lifted up the humble.*
> *He has filled the hungry with good things but has sent the rich away empty.*
> *He has helped his servant Israel, remembering to be merciful to Abraham and his descendants forever, even as he said to our fathers.*
> *Luke 1: 46-55*

This inspired passage ranks among the most enchanting poetry in Scripture. What is truly astounding is that Luke reports it to be Mary's spontaneous response to the prophetic word of a relative. We call it the *Magnificat* based on the opening words that magnify (glorify) God as used in the old Latin translation. This oration is valuable in what it suggests about Mary herself as well as what it tells us about God and his redemptive plan.

Scholars tend to believe that Mary was a very young woman, an adolescent, perhaps only sixteen years of age at the birth of Christ. This corresponds with the fact that she was still alive three decades later at Jesus' crucifixion. Shortly before proclaiming the Magnificat, an angel told her that she would give birth to a son, although she was unmarried and had never had sexual relations with a man. After facing her fiancé with this unexpected news, she traveled to visit her cousin Elisabeth, who was probably more of an aunt-figure to Mary due to the disparity in their ages. The angel had told Mary that Elisabeth too was to have a child—Elisabeth's first after a lifetime of barrenness. When Mary entered the house and greeted her, Elisabeth responded with the following prophetic blessing:

> Blessed are you among women, and blessed is the child that you will bear. But why am I so favored that the mother of my Lord should come to me? As soon as the sound of your greeting reached my ears, the baby in my womb leaped for joy. Blessed is she who has believed that what the Lord has said to her will be accomplished![14]

Mary replied, "My soul glorifies the Lord!"

Elisabeth's exclamation, and the entirety of their interaction, reveals a key feature of Mary's character: faith. When told of her pending, supernatural pregnancy by the angel, Mary responded "let it be to me as you say." Elisabeth, inspired by the Holy Spirit, commends this faith in her protégé: "blessed is she who has believed." Moreover, in Mary's testimony, she has accepted her role: "he has done great things to me." Mary em-

---

[14] Luke 1:42-45.

braced her destiny in faith, believing that God would do as he said and accepting that he had chosen her for this mission. She did not dither, as Moses did when he was commissioned, nor did she reject the calling, as did Jonah—she accepted her own cross, a lifetime experience that Simeon prophesied a month later would cause her heart to be pierced as with a sword.

The Magnificat demonstrates that Mary was also humble. To both the angel and to Elisabeth Mary refers to herself as a "handmaid." This term would be better translated today as "servant" or "slave" and clearly represents the meekness and low estate of the person so described. Mary's was not false modesty—as far as we can ascertain, Mary never went on to fame, wealth, or ease during her lifetime. Undoubtedly her reputation remained suspect because there were those who never believed anything but scandal regarding Jesus' origins. Mary lived much of her adult life in the most provincial of settings. Moreover, we have no record of her pressuring her son to assert his kingship, unlike the wife of Zebedee who urged her sons, James and John, to ask Christ to seat them on thrones next to his own in heaven. In fact, the only miracle that we know she asked for was for Jesus to save a wedding party from the embarrassment of not providing enough provisions for their guests. In sum, because Mary had fully surrendered her life to her God as a bond servant to her Master, she was able to humbly accept her role as a participant in the Christmas story.

The Magnificat's text suggests that Mary was very knowledgeable of Scripture. Scholars assert that there are as many as fifteen Old Testament references or quotations in the Magnificat. In other words, this lovely poetry was spontaneously adapted and quoted from Old Testament writings by the aid of the Holy Spirit. This probably means that Mary came from a home that venerated the Scripture as the living word of Jehovah God and that she had memorized or was familiar with key passages. Certainly, divine inspiration played a part in uttering this heavenly verse, but Mary's tongue was expressing what was already in her heart: "from the abundance of the heart, the mouth speaks."[15]

Finally, Mary took the long-view of things. She had to have known that most people around her, even her closest friends and relatives, were most likely to shun and condemn her as an adulteress, at least at first. Imagine if your daughter came to you, a month or two prior to her nuptials, and said, "Father, I am pregnant…by the Holy Spirit of God." Those around her were likely fixated on the present state of affairs: "How do we fix this?" "Be honest, was it Joseph or is there someone else?" "An angel came to you, oh really?" "What will the neighbors say? What will your grandfather say?!" However, Mary trusted that it would be to her just as the angel foretold. She knew that her faith would be vindicated over time. Indeed, Mary proudly claimed that "future generations will call me blessed."

The passage tells us at least two things about God's nature: he is both powerful and merciful. Mary testifies of the awesome power and majesty of Creator God, who judges mankind and oversees the affairs of the world. To the Jewish hearer, this immediately brought to mind the Exodus, God's provision in the Promised Land, and the golden age of David's kingdom. This is not the Watchmaker god of deism who wound up the universe and now is distant, this is an active, participant, engaged Deity. Furthermore, the omnipotence of God can be extended in blessing to the humble and to the poor, but can be directed against the pretensions of the rich and the proud.

A second theme is the mercy of God. It is God's unmerited favor that allowed a sinful woman, in most ways like any other young lady, to conceive the Son of God. It is the mercy of God, not deserved justice or punishment, that induces him to send a Savior to atone for our sins. Additionally, it is the merci-

---

[15] Matthew 12:34.

ful nature of God that guides salvation history to provide redemption time and again to Abraham's descendants and beyond. Indeed this mercy extends to all who reverence ("fear") him: "For God so loved the world that he gave his only Son, that whosoever believes on him shall not perish..."[16]

The song of Mary reminds us that God is faithful to his promises and that he is merciful to those who trust him. Moreover, Mary's example of faith and humility, grounded in a personal relationship with God and a knowledge of the Holy Scripture, is a model for us when life is tough or others mock the promise God has given to our hearts.

---

[16] John 3:16.

Chapter 14

The Second Adam

The Lord God formed Adam from the dust of the ground and breathed into his nostrils the breath of life, and the man became a living being.
Genesis 2:7

For if, by the trespass of the one man [Adam], death reigned through that one man, how much more will those who receive God's abundant provision of grace and of the gift of righteousness reign in life through the one man, Jesus Christ. Romans 5:17

So it is written: "The first man became a living being," the last Adam, a life-giving spirit…the first man was of the dust of the earth, the second man from heaven. As was the earthly man, so are those who are of the earth; and as is the man from heaven, so also are those who are of heaven.
1 Corinthians 15:45

The Bible begins with the creation of a man, the first man, Adam. Adam was created in the image of God: he was a "living being" animated by the breath of God. This made him radically different from the rest of creation. Adam's purpose was to be in relationship to God as only sentient moral beings can be—building friendship based on free will and mutual respect. Adam also had a job to do, to superintend his vast dominion as the viceroy of the Creator, and to do so with integrity and diligence.

Adam failed. He chose to transgress the trust placed in him by his God and friend, and instead of stewarding the Garden in his care, he did nothing to stop an evil force from entering his domain. Adam did not intervene to protect his mate from temptation; he apparently watched silently. At the crucial moment of leadership, he abdicated responsibility and deliberately chose the single act that would cut his descendants off from face-to-face relationship with God.

Despite this, and the centuries of human sin that intervened between the Fall of man and the advent of the Messiah, God did not forget the human beings that he created. The Old Testament testifies that God loved the world so much that he intervened in various times and places to try to steer mankind back on track. He did so in various empires of old—ancient Babel, Noah's pre-diluvian society, to the Mesopotamian family of Terah, to the Semitic descendants of Abraham that inhabit today's Middle East, to Job and his descendants, to the Egyptians through Joseph, the Assyrians through Jonah, and to both the Babylonians and Persians through Daniel. God's response of love and forgiveness to humans sin has been repeated countless times, but always as a promise—that God would send the ultimate gift to forgive humanity of its sins.

That gift was a second Adam—Jesus. The first Adam was created when light came out of darkness and God's spirit hovered over the primeval world, "Let there be light!" The second Adam also arrived in a world shrouded by spiritual darkness, birthed in the dark of night on the frontier of an ungodly empire to unknown parents. The first Adam became truly alive when God himself breathed life into his nostrils. The second Adam was similarly generated by the agency of God—it was God's life force that supernaturally entered the womb of a virgin, causing an egg to be divinely fertilized and resulting in DNA untainted by Adam's sin. God said that the first Adam was in his very own image; God said that the second Adam was his one true son.

To the first Adam God gave a responsibility: be fruitful, multiply, and take dominion over the earth. God likewise charged the second Adam with a global responsibility: redeem the planet for me. Through the first Adam sin entered the world as he willing, deliberately, knowingly, and intentionally observed his wife speaking with the Serpent, declined to intervene, handled the forbidden fruit, examined it, smelled it, and bit deeply into it...calculatingly forsaking his birthright, perhaps in hope of transcending his heavenly father.

The second Adam had every opportunity to turn away from the road before him. At any point of his adult ministry he could have given into vanity or to the temptation to use his powers to harm his enemies. The Bible says that he was tempted in all points as we are, so it is likely that at times the second Adam was tempted to look on a beautiful woman with lust, to covet the wealth that would bring deserved ease, or simply to tell a white lie. Satan tempted Jesus to take the easy road to earthly success and power early in his ministry. And at the end of his life he was tempted to forsake his role as the second Adam in a second Garden: he cried out, "Lord, please take this cup [my destiny to die] from me..."

Yet the second Adam went on to say, "...but not my will, but Yours be done." This obedience to the purpose laid out for him by his heavenly father made the second Adam victorious in a way that the first Adam could only bitterly reflect on in the centuries that passed before his death. The second Adam succeeded in re-establishing God's spiritual purity and right relationship in the hearts of human beings through the sacrifice made at Calvary.

Hence, the Christmas story that appears to begin at a stable in Bethlehem is really the second chapter, or an alternative ending, to the Creation story that began in Genesis. It is the climax of a lengthy saga recording God's eternal love for humanity: the birth of a new Adam who brings hope and redemption to us all:

For God so loved the world, that he gave his only begotten son, that whosoever believes in him shall not perish, but have everlasting life.[17]

---

[17] John 3:16.

Chapter 15

Zechariah's Prophecy and God's Mercy

When it was time for Elisabeth to have her baby, she gave birth to a son. Her neighbors and relatives heard that the Lord had shown her great mercy, and they shared her joy. On the eighth day they came to circumcise the child, and they were going to name him after his father Zechariah, but his mother spoke up and said, "No! He is to be called John." They said to her, "There is no one among your relatives who has that name." Then they made signs to his father, to find out what he would like to name the child. He asked for a writing tablet, and to everyone's astonishment he wrote, "His name is John." Immediately his mouth was opened and his tongue loosed, and he began to speak, praising God. The neighbors were all filled with awe, and throughout the hill country of Judea people were talking about all these things. Everyone who heard this wondered about it, asking, "What then is this child going to be?" For the Lord's hand was with him. His father Zechariah was filled with the Holy Spirit and prophesied,

> *'Praise be to the Lord, the God of Israel, because he has come and has redeemed his people. He has raised up a horn of salvation for us in the house of his servant David (as he said through his holy prophets of long ago), salvation from our enemies and from the hand of all who hate us—*
> *to show mercy to our fathers and to remember his holy covenant, the oath he swore to our father Abraham: to rescue us from the hand of our enemies, and to enable us to serve him without fear in holiness and righteousness before him all our days.*

> *And you, my child, will be called a prophet of the Most High; for you will go on before the Lord to prepare the way for him, to give his people the knowledge of salvation through the forgiveness of their sins, because of the tender mercy of our God, by which the rising sun will come to us from heaven to shine on those living in darkness and in the shadow of death, and to guide our feet into the path of peace.* Luke 1:57-79

Elisabeth, Zechariah, and their neighbors and relatives knew that the gift of a son at their advanced age was an act of "great mercy." They were humbled and joyful because it was a gift of supernatural grace—it was undeserved and unexpected. Moreover, the miracle was apparently known throughout the area and therefore the happiness and wonder was widely shared.

The cornerstone of this passage is Zechariah's prophecy, which is prefaced by two questions. The first question is most obvious: "What will you name him [their newborn son]?" Zechariah's friends and neighbors were shocked when Elisabeth responded, "John," because this was not a family name and therefore was socially inappropriate. Seeing that they could not sway Elisabeth's resolution, the crowd turned to Zechariah, assuming that he would override his wife. Interestingly, "they made signs to" Zechariah, rather than spoke to him. This suggests that in addition to being struck mute by the angel Gabriel for his unbelief, Zechariah was simultaneously rendered deaf. Of course, it is also possible that at his advanced age his hearing was failing naturally. Either way, Zechariah would have been difficult to communicate with over the previous nine months assuming that he was both deaf and dumb.

"What will you name him?" To the people's chagrin, Zechariah seconded his wife in writing, "John." This was the name that the angel commanded nearly a year earlier. It is likely that Zechariah, though mute at the angel's touch due to his disbelief, had nonetheless communicated this name to Elisabeth and thus they were united in obedience and thanksgiving to God. Moreover, John was a perfect name for their miracle child as it means "Jehovah shows favor."

With the baby's birth and his obedient affirmation of Gabriel's command to name the child John, Zechariah' speech returned and he immediately began praising God. The neighbors likewise thanked God for this turn of events, and many pondered the significance, asking a second question, "What then is this child going to be?"

The second question, that of John's destiny, is deeply significant. This question sets the backdrop for Zechariah' prophecy, a message rooted in Old Testament images that speaks to the past, present, and future of God's redemptive plan.

Modern readers often breeze past the second question and the accompanying prophecy. This is perhaps natural because the very next passage records the birth of Christ, with the memorable introduction, "And it came to pass in those days, that there went out a decree from Caesar Augustus..." For the casual observer, the Christmas story begins with Caesar's decree that "all the world should be taxed." However, the author, Luke, writing decades later, thought differently. Not only did he carefully record Zechariah's prophecy, but he also provided a deliberate answer to the second question: "What then is this child going to be?" Luke answered, "The Lord's hand was with him." On the day of John's birth, Zechariah provided an answer to the second question. His response was inspired by the Holy Spirit and asserted that his son was simply another instrument of God's grace and redemption. The sub-text to the prophecy is that throughout history Israel had fallen away from God time and again, only to be forgiven by a merciful Father each time conditions got so bad that Israel returned to the true faith. Israel was then enduring a period of 400 "silent years" during which no new prophetic voice had been heard, but during which the Jewish people had been ruled by a succession of pagan foreign governments: the Babylonians, the Persians, the Greeks, and the Romans. And due to Israel's track record of sin, they certainly deserved nothing better.

But Zechariah trumpeted the mercy of God who had promised to absolve the sinner and redeem Israel. God was merciful in upholding and enacting his end of the bargain that Israel had violated over and over again. Most importantly, God's mercy was going to provide spiritual forgiveness, characterized as a "rising sun" illuminating the life of those "living in darkness," with hope and love and setting Israel on "the path of peace." Such mercy is available to all who turn their lives over to Christ and actively believe in his mercy.

Zechariah began, "Blessed is the Lord...for He has visited and redeemed his people and raised up a horn of salvation for us in the house of...David." Horns represent power and thus were associated with kingship, and in this case the horn may represent both the authority of Messiah as well as be symbolic of a vessel holding the anointing oil for purification and anointing. Zechariah is pointing out that after centuries of bondage, loss, and silence—that God had finally spoken overtly to Israel and that this baby would be a similar voice. Verse 69 also told them that deliverance was imminent, that God had "raised up" a vessel of salvation from the house of David. In other words, the kingly line was to produce an heir that would bring deliverance—this is an explicit Messianic statement of hope and redemption.

Zechariah also reminded them of the terms of the Jewish covenant: salvation from their enemies, that they might "serve God without fear in righteousness and holiness all the days of [y]our life." Such salvation was clearly spiritual, because it included the "remission of their sins through the tender mercy of God." It is important to note that Zechariah's prophecy says nothing about the all powerful God overthrowing the Romans and setting up a hegemonic Jewish state. Instead, the message intimated that God's ultimate desire was to cleanse the hearts of his people of their sinfulness and draw them into intimacy with himself.

Of course, Zechariah was also reminding them that it was not God who had abrogated the terms of the covenant—time and again it had been the Israelites who had done so. Nevertheless, God once again is promising mercy and love to those who will give themselves to his heavenly relationship.

The passage concludes that "the rising sun will come to us from heaven to shine on those living in darkness and in the shadow of death, and to guide our feet into the path of peace." Again, this beautiful image of celestial light beaming down and illuminating the dark planet is directly from the Old Testament. The prophet Micah had written four centuries earlier, "But for you who revere my name, the sun of righteousness will rise with healing in its wings." And of course, the twenty-third Psalm testifies that "even in the valley of the shadow of death," we need not fear because God will protect us.[18]

In short, the people asked what kind of child this will be. Zechariah answered: "And you, my child, will be called a prophet of the Most High; for you will go on before the Lord to prepare the way for him." This child, John, would be a living testimony of God's grace and mercy and that his life message would point to God's love and desire to bring salvation to them through the person of another baby born that year—Jesus Christ. And the beauty of this passage still attracts our attention today, both because of the imagery and the prose, but also due to its message: that God sent his son to bring light and redemption to our lives.

---

[18] Micah 4:2; Psalm 23:3.

Chapter 16

The Genealogies of the Christ

A record of the genealogy of Jesus Christ the son of David, the son of Abraham: Abraham was the father of Isaac, Isaac the father of Jacob, Jacob the father of Judah and his brothers, Judah the father of Perez and Zerah, whose mother was Tamar, Perez the father of Hezron, Hezron the father of Ram, Ram the father of Amminadab, Amminadab the father of Nahshon, Nahshon the father of Salmon, Salmon the father of Boaz, whose mother was Rahab, Boaz the father of Obed, whose mother was Ruth, Obed the father of Jesse, and Jesse the father of King David. David was the father of Solomon, whose mother had been Uriah's wife, Solomon the father of Rehoboam, Rehoboam the father of Abijah, Abijah the father of Asa, Asa the father of Jehoshaphat, Jehoshaphat the father of Jehoram, Jehoram the father of Uzziah, Uzziah the father of Jotham, Jotham the father of Ahaz, Ahaz the father of Hezekiah, Hezekiah the father of Manasseh, Manasseh the father of Amon, Amon the father of Josiah, and Josiah the father of Jeconiah and his brothers at the time of the exile to Babylon. After the exile to Babylon: Jeconiah was the father of Shealtiel, Shealtiel the father of Zerubbabel, Zerubbabel the father of Abiud, Abiud the father of Eliakim, Eliakim the father of Azor, Azor the father of Zadok, Zadok the father of Akim, Akim the father of Eliud, Eliud the father of Eleazar, Eleazar the father of Matthan, Matthan the father of Jacob, and Jacob the father of Joseph, the husband of Mary, of whom was born Jesus, who is called Christ. Matthew 1:1-17

Now Jesus himself was about thirty years old when he began his ministry. He was the son, so it was thought, of Joseph, the son of Heli, the son of Matthat, the son of Levi, the son of Melki, the son of Jannai, the son of

Joseph, the son of Mattathias, the son of Amos, the son of Nahum, the son of Esli, the son of Naggai, the son of Maath, the son of Mattathias, the son of Semein, the son of Josech, the son of Joda, the son of Joanan, the son of Rhesa, the son of Zerubbabel, the son of Shealtiel, the son of Neri, the son of Melki, the son of Addi, the son of Cosam, the son of Elmadam, the son of Er, the son of Joshua, the son of Eliezer, the son of Jorim, the son of Matthat, the son of Levi, the son of Simeon, the son of Judah, the son of Joseph, the son of Jonam, the son of Eliakim, the son of Melea, the son of Menna, the son of Mattatha, the son of Nathan, the son of David, the son of Jesse, the son of Obed, the son of Boaz, the son of Salmon, the son of Nahshon, the son of Amminadab, the son of Ram, the son of Hezron, the son of Perez, the son of Judah, the son of Jacob, the son of Isaac, the son of Abraham, the son of Terah, the son of Nahor, the son of Serug, the son of Reu, the son of Peleg, the son of Eber, the son of Shelah, the son of Cainan, the son of Arphaxad, the son of Shem, the son of Noah, the son of Lamech, the son of Methuselah, the son of Enoch, the son of Jared, the son of Mahalalel, the son of Kenan, the son of Enosh, the son of Seth, the son of Adam, the son of God. Luke 3:23-37

The Gospels of Matthew and Luke begin with long genealogical reports, recording the lineage of Jesus through his parents back via King David to the patriarchs at the mists of Jewish history. The genealogies are formal, repetitive affairs, "Zerubabel was the father of..." Nonetheless, these records establish Jesus' claim to David's throne and are testimonials to the faithfulness and mercy of God.

Even a cursory scrutiny of the two passages reveals that the genealogies are not identical. How can this be? Scholars believe that one of the genealogies, the one in Matthew's Gospel, provides the ancestry of Christ's mother Mary. This line runs from David through Solomon and Rehoboam through the kings of Judah, ultimately surviving attacks and/or enslavement by Egyptians, Assyrians, Babylonians, Medo-Persians, Greeks, and the

Romans. A repository of this royal bloodline is a humble young woman, barely more than a girl, Mary.

In contrast, scholars believe that the Lucan genealogy is that of Jesus' earthly, but not biological, father Joseph. Joseph was also of the Davidic line, but through a different son of David, and was therefore ineligible for kingship.

It is doubtful that the people of Jesus' day venerated Mary and her family members as royalty-in-waiting: Israel had experienced too many historic disappointments and had apparently resigned itself to spiritual independence within political subservience. Indeed, a century and a half before Christ when the Jews had rallied against their Hellenistic oppressors, they rallied around individuals with religious credentials, or better religio-nationalist zeal, to protect their unique culture and religion.

Nevertheless, the genealogy of Christ reminds us of his rightful claim to David's throne. Moreover, it demonstrates for us the care that God took over the centuries to protect and preserve David's line, as God had promised David that he would do. The birth of Jesus, conceived of divine matter within an heiress of David, created in Jesus the only person who would be able to live up to the prophecies of the Old Testament.

The genealogy also tells us of God's faithfulness to his people Israel over the long centuries of disobedience. It was the patriarchs who from time to time turned their backs on God (e.g. Lot, Esau). It was the Israelites, not God, who broke the covenant time and again in the books of Judges and the royal histories. It was David's descendants, beginning with his son Solomon, who repeatedly turned Israel to idolatry and immorality—even child sacrifice—in gross violation of the redemptive Judaic covenant. And through it all—slavery, warfare, defeat, sinfulness—God renewed his relationship with the people of Israel again and again. God was ready to impart forgiveness and relationship to any individual and to any generation that was willing to embrace him as Lord.

The genealogy reminds us that God carefully preserved the line of Abraham and of David, against all historical odds, for his purpose. In the course of millennia, other families die out or are wiped out, but Jesus' antecedents maintained virility over the centuries. God preserved the Hebrews despite bondage in Egypt, hostile neighbors in Canaan, and the depredations of barbaric nomads during the time of the Judges. Later, the Davidic line fought a civil war against itself, fought and lost against much mightier armies, saw some of its kings and princes dragged off in chains to captivity, and was scattered across the Middle East. Nonetheless, God preserved, nourished, and protected this family so that its greatest son could be born to save the world from its sin.

The genealogy also should remind us that God loves sinners and will use imperfect vessels to do his will. David's royal tribe is that of Judah, and Jesus is directly descended from Judah's incestuous relationship with his own daughter-in-law. Similarly, in a nation where purity of blood was paramount and Gentiles were restricted in their approach to God within the Jewish community, God used godly, non-Jewish women to provide strength to Jesus' line, most notably the prostitute Rahab of Canaan and Ruth the Moabitess. Moreover, Jesus' forbears had closetfuls of skeletons, most notoriously David's illicit affair with Bathsheba and murder of her husband as well as the wickedness of Manasseh and a dozen other licentious, idol-worshipping kings.

Nonetheless, through it all God preserved the heritage of Abraham and of David, to rise again and again in people of faith such as Boaz and Ruth, Salmon and Rahab, Obed, Jesse, and a dozen righteous monarchs such as Asa and Hezekiah. God was faithful to his promise to Abraham to preserve and grow this people, and God honored his promise to David to preserve his line including a future king with ultimate power. And God brought all of this together in a young woman named Mary who had a baby she named Jesus.

We stand reminded that God takes the long view of human affairs and that he is faithful to his promise of blessing and solidarity with those who love and honor him. Just as a young Jesus could probably recite his family tree and with pride look on God's blessings to his ancestors, so we too should take occasion to look over our shoulder and testify regarding how God has had an invisible hand in our own past, ultimately bringing us to individual salvation in Christ's name.

Chapter 17

The Consolation of Israel

"He was waiting for the consolation of Israel..." Luke 2:25

Psychologists tell us that the time of the year that individuals are most depressed and most likely to commit suicide is during the Christmas season. The compressed calendar of traditional family holidays (Thanksgiving, Christmas, New Year's Day) can cause tremendous pain to those who have had terrible family experiences or to those who have lost family members and retain only the memories of better times. Moreover, the pressures caused by poor weather, unhealthy eating, increased alcohol consumption, chaotic schedules, and the like can make December a dangerous month.

What many of us are looking for during this bittersweet period is "consolation." It is interesting that this word is used once in the Christmas story, to describe a venerable but aged prophet awaiting the "consolation of Israel" in the person of the Messiah. The concept of consolation is important, because Christ later taught that he would send a "consoler" when his ministry ended.

The passage from the Christmas story simply says that Simeon was waiting for the consolation of Israel. The Greek word translated "consolation" is *paraklesis*, and can also be translated "comfort" or "exhort." A more literal translation means "calling to one's side" (para=beside, kaleo=to call). A closely related word is *parakletos*, which is translated as "one who comes alongside" or "advocate." *Parakletos* has the connotation of legal assistance, as the defense counsel or advocate for the accused. In a sense, the *parakletos* is both a comfort to the accused as well as an intercessor on their behalf. [19]

Consequently, the phrase "Simeon was waiting for the consolation of Israel…" is rich with meaning, particularly as the notion of "consolation" and "the Comforter" appears in both the writings of Luke and John.

Literally, Simeon was waiting for the consolation of Israel in the person of the Jewish Messiah. A country that had groaned under foreign oppression and spiritless religious ritual was in dire need for the succor of the Savior. The Jewish nation, and in fact the entire world, needed the completing work of Christ as Savior in order to bring to salvation history to its consummation. Simeon was spiritually aware enough to tangibly feel the terrible lostness of the human race and yet hope for the appearance of God's Messiah. When he encountered Jesus, he knew in his spirit that God had honored His promise to bring the ultimate advocate to the human race.

During his ministry, Jesus picked up the theme of *paraklesis/parakletos*. John records a long session spanning more than one chapter when Jesus was training his disciples. Jesus directly spoke about the coming of "another" Comforter to minister to his followers:

> If you love me, you will obey what I command. And I will ask the Father, and he will give you another Counselor [*parakletos*] to be with you forever—the Spirit of truth.
>
> But the Counselor, the Holy Spirit, whom the Father will send in my name, will teach you all things and will remind you of everything I have said to you.

---

[19] See Vine's Expository Dictionary, pp. 110-111.

> When the Counselor comes, whom I will send to you from the Father, the Spirit of truth who goes out from the Father, he will testify about me.
>
> But I tell you the truth: it is for your good that I am going away. Unless I go away, the Counselor will not come to you, but if I go, I will send him to you.[20]

It is intriguing to consider what Jesus taught about a consoler/counselor/comforter because it directly reflects not only the advent of the Holy Spirit following his ascension, but also on the nature of Christ's ministry while he was here on earth. Did Simeon's hope for the consolation of Israel correspond to Christ's teaching about divine advocacy?

Jesus' words from John's Gospel direct us to love God first and foremost. Christ abjured us that those who love God follow God's commands. In order to provide assistance in doing so, Jesus promised to send the Counselor to be with us forever. Christ also called this Counselor the Spirit of truth, meaning that the *parakletos* will serve as an advocate of the believer before God but also assist the Christian in discerning right and wrong in this life. This form of intimacy seems to have characterized the life of Simeon, and his prophecy asserted that such relationship was possible for a much broader spectrum of humanity than just himself—Israel could be consoled and made spiritually healthy.

The second and third verses speak of the operative agency of the Comforter. When Christ was pursuing his earthly ministry, he was a teacher above all. His instruction focused on directing people to God and reminding them of the countless evidences of God's love for humanity in the Old Testament. Similarly, Jesus pointed to the future work of the Comforter, exhorting the Church to recall and embrace Christ's saving work.

---

[20] These four quotes are from John 14:15-16, 14:26, 15:26, and 16:7.

The final verse is ironic, because Simeon waited a lifetime to see the consolation of Israel and in a metaphorical sense, the Jewish nation had been waiting centuries to experience the consolation associated with the physical advent of the Messiah. However, Christ said that he must leave in order for the Counselor to come. This demonstrates that the Christmas story was the beginning, not the ending, of the next phase of God's intercessory work on behalf of humankind.

In sum, a wizened patriarch spent his life faithfully waiting for the coming of a Messiah who would bring wholeness to the world. That Messiah was Jesus Christ, whose atoning death and resurrection interceded on behalf of humanity before a just but loving God, advocating mercy and redemption. In this sense Christ was the first *parakletos*, but Jesus went on to teach that the reality of God's presence would be universal with the coming of the Holy Spirit directly into the lives of believers. This consolation would be global in effect, as the Holy Spirit comes alongside all who are willing to be comforted and exhorted by God's Spirit. This is a message of holiday hope—that the consolation of history is found in the Spirit of God, available to all who trust in the name of Jesus Christ as Lord.

Chapter 18

Mary: Heroic and Human

In the sixth month, God sent the angel Gabriel to Nazareth, to a town in Galilee, to a virgin pledged to be married to a man named Joseph, a descendant of David. The virgin's name was Mary. The angel went to her and said, "Greetings, you who are highly favored! The Lord is with you." Mary was greatly troubled at his words and wondered what kind of greeting this might be. But the angel said to her, "Do not be afraid, Mary, you have found favor with God. You will be with child and give birth to a son, and you are to give him the name Jesus. He will be great and will be called the Son of the Most High. The Lord God will give him the throne of his father David, and he will reign over the house of Jacob forever; his kingdom will never end." "How will this be," Mary asked the angel, "since I am a virgin?" The angel answered, "The Holy Spirit will come upon you, and the power of the Most High will overshadow you. So the holy one to be born will be called the Son of God. Even Elisabeth your relative is going to have a child in her old age, and she who was said to be barren is in her sixth month. For nothing is impossible with God." I am the Lord's servant," Mary answered. "May it be to me as you have said." Then the angel left her. Luke 1:26-38

This is how the birth of Jesus Christ came about: his mother Mary was pledged to be married to Joseph, but before they came together, she was found to be with child through the Holy Spirit. Because Joseph her husband was a righteous man and did not want to expose her to public disgrace, he had in mind to divorce her quietly. Matthew 1:18-19

There is tremendous confusion regarding the character of the mother of Christ and what lessons we should draw from her example. For instance, there are those who speculate that she was a young maiden of fourteen or fifteen years of age during these events, with all of the simplicity that age suggests—even in a culture when women married young and life expectancy for females was in the late thirties. Such a view contrasts an adolescent Mary with an older Joseph: a man of more experience and worldly wisdom. In short, a common portrait of Mary is as a demure, innocent, gentle, and rustic teenager, thrust into these events, in part, due to her innate naïveté.

In contrast, many in Christendom have exalted the position of Mary from mother of baby Jesus, to Queen of Heaven, doer of miracles, a vision for the desperate, and an intermediary between the earth's miserable and her aloof son. In such a view she is wise and powerful: the matriarch of the universe.

Perhaps neither perspective is accurate. Certainly the Scripture gives us barely enough to complete a portrait. In contrast to the two icons above, Mary may just as easily have been a patriotic young woman, proud of her race and of her family's princely lineage. Undoubtedly she would have been aware that she was a daughter in King David's royal family. Rather than being passive and dull, the passages above suggest that she quickly grasped the essentials of her situation through faith and common sense: "God has made a promise to me…what about Joseph?" The passage from Matthew indicates that her first act is taken with a decisiveness and courage that bespeaks a clean conscience and strength of character: she openly confronted Joseph with the information that she was pregnant. It is only after that she told Joseph and he considered divorcing her quietly, that he was visited by an angel who confirmed Mary's testimony.

Mary's next step seems equally purposeful: she immediately departs to visit her aged but pregnant cousin Elisabeth. The question is, did Mary go to the home of Elisabeth to verify the angel's story, or did Mary visit Elisabeth believing the good news in faith with the intention of celebrating with Elisabeth? Everything indicates that Mary accepted the angelic message for her own life, and so she certainly would have believed that her cousin was similarly experiencing the miraculous.

Indeed, Elisabeth's testimony regarding Mary affirmed this. When Mary reached the doorway to Elisabeth's home, the latter was filled with the Spirit and cried out prophetically, "Blessed is she who believed that what the Lord has said to her will be accomplished." God's choice for Jesus' mother was a person who could accept God's massive promise on God's terms.

Interestingly, Mary arrived at Elisabeth's home during the sixth month of the latter's pregnancy and stayed for three months. We know little about the particulars of their time together. Elisabeth's household may have supported the younger woman during the first trimester with its accompanying morning sickness and physical changes. Or perhaps, Mary provided both comfort and domestic assistance to Elisabeth through the birth of John the Baptist. In any event, Mary was located in an environment of faith that would strengthen her for the road ahead.

In short, Mary's core character was defined by personal integrity and robust faith. Hers was not the type of vague, mystical belief in an impersonal religious system that would shrivel under hardship, for difficulties she was to endure. Although Joseph, Zechariah, and Elisabeth must have come to believe fully in the supernaturality of the virgin birth, Mary had to have faced all sorts of mockery and scorn over her pre-marital pregnancy. Imagine how mean small-town gossips must have been to Mary in her home village! Did her father believe Mary's wild tale of an angelic male visitor to her bedroom in the middle of the night? Did her mother? Her brothers and sisters? Mary had to endure all of this with the assistance of God's Spirit and her beloved Joseph, himself the butt of jokes or derision.

Mary must have been a thoughtful, engaged, spiritual, and intelligent adult. Her beautiful Magnificat indicates a rich knowledge of Scripture and wellsprings of love for God. She appears to be humble when presented with a divine commission, but not faint-hearted. She must have been strong without haughtiness and self-confident without conceit. If we knew her personally, we would probably consider her to be energetic, wise for her years, righteous, and resolute—the qualities necessary to absorb the reality of this bizarre set of events as well as thrive during the flight to Egypt, life in a foreign country, and the uncertain days ahead for her special child.

What should we learn from Mary? She is a biblical heroine, not a passive ingénue. She was with Jesus from before his birth through his crucifixion, burial, and resurrection. We should emulate her faith—a faith that overcame the doubts of others and the death of her firstborn. We should acknowledge her obedience and commit to doing likewise when directed by God. We should learn from her thoughtfulness, for we know that she kept the early prophecies and experiences in her heart throughout her life. And we should learn from her bravery, the courage that comes from a clean conscience and rootedness in Christian faith.

Chapter 19

Joseph the Dreamer

...the angel of the Lord appeared to him in a dream, saying, "Joseph, son of David, fear not to take Mary as your wife, for what is conceived in her is of the Holy Spirit. She will give birth to a son, and you are to give him the name Jesus, because he will save his people from their sins..." When Joseph woke up he did what the angel of the Lord had commanded him, and took Mary home as his wife. Matthew 1:20-24

When they [the Magi] had gone, an angel of the Lord appeared to Joseph in a dream. "Get up," he said, "take the child and his mother and escape to Egypt. Stay there until I tell you, for Herod is going to search for the child to kill him." So he got up, took the child and his mother during the night and left for Egypt....After Herod died, an angel of the Lord appeared in a dream to Joseph in Egypt, and said, "Get up, take the child and his mother, and go to the land of Israel, for those who were trying to take the child's life are dead." So he got up, took the child and his mother, and went to the land of Israel. Matthew 2: 13-14, 19-21

The Church has historically focused its attention almost solely on Mary rather than drawing lessons from the example of Joseph. Of course, the role of Christ's mother is worthy of our attention and respect, but we should not entirely neglect Joseph, although there is far less scriptural material directly relating to him. These passages from the Christmas story, as told by Matthew, clarify Joseph's role as head of his household and identify him as spiritually sensitive and obedient to the will of God. Joseph is also representative of numerous characters in the

Christmas story whose faith epitomized the spiritual maxim that "believing is seeing."

First, we should consider the character of Joseph. He was the kind of man that the virgin mother of Christ could depend upon as a spouse and life partner. At that time, it would have been natural for the marriage to have been arranged between Mary's parents and Joseph, or between both sets of parents. However, this does not necessarily mean that Joseph and Mary were strangers. Assuming that they were both from the modest village of Nazareth, it is likely that they knew each other and desired the match. Thus, when we recognize the obvious character strengths of Mary, we have a reflection of the man of integrity that Joseph must have been.

Beyond Mary's confidence in and compatibility with this man, we have the far more important recommendation of God himself: it was our heavenly Father who selected this man, out of the billions in human history, to act as the adopted father to Jesus Christ. What kind of man would the Creator God choose to raise his only begotten Son? Certainly one of moral courage, personal righteousness, and spiritual maturity. Most importantly, God must have known of Joseph's unconditional surrender to God's will.

Regardless of the angelic visits, it is clear that Joseph also took his religious obligations seriously. In addition to obeying the secular laws of the day by traveling to Bethlehem with a near-term pregnant wife, he also fulfilled the demands of his Jewish faith by circumcising Jesus on the eighth day and then traveling to the temple for the child's consecration on the fortieth day following Jesus' birth. It is probably safe to say that Joseph similarly fulfilled the rest of his religious duties on a regular basis, from the Passover feast to the appointed sacrifices to regular synagogue attendance.

In short, before the supernatural visitations recounted in Matthew's text, Joseph was undoubtedly a man of integrity and spirituality. He may have been a quiet, reflective man or he may have been the life of the party: we simply do not know. However, on at least three occasions he was directly visited by an angel during his sleep. The first time followed on the heels of a strange conversation with his betrothed. Mary had just told him that she was pregnant. She claimed that this pregnancy was the result of supernatural agency, and although she did not yet "feel" a child within her, she believed the promise given her by an angelic messenger. Joseph must have been stunned, and Matthew reports that Joseph seriously considered terminating their engagement. However, upon the angelic revelation that this was truly of God, Joseph took Mary as his wife.

It should be noted that we have no record of Joseph arguing with the angel, as in the case of Zechariah when he learned of the miraculous pregnancy of Elisabeth. Moreover, in all three of Joseph's recorded angelic encounters we have no hint that Joseph disbelieved or questioned the angel. Joseph did not awake the next morning and discount his experience as "just a dream." The angel said, "Take Mary to wife." Joseph did. The angel said, "Flee!" Joseph did. The angel said, "Return." Joseph did.

Joseph believed, acted, and then saw the fruit of that belief. His example is representative of a larger pattern in the Christmas story—God kept asking people to believe and act appropriately. In contrast to the "seeing is believing" of the skeptics, God called on the actors in this drama to obey his directives to participate in a supernatural event: believe and see! Not only did Joseph respond in faith, but so too did an entire cast of characters. Mary believed the angel and went to Joseph, confessing her pre-marital pregnancy with no certainty that he would accept her. The shepherds were woken in the night and told to find a king in a stable, and they followed the angel's summons to a baby lying in a feeding trough. They then went out and spread the good news of what they had seen.

The Magi received some sort of astrological oracle and traveled across Mesopotamia, and perhaps farther, to the center of the crude Jewish civilization, seeking the Son of God. Elisabeth believed that the baby inside her was the new Elijah, and more importantly, that her young cousin Mary was to mother the Messiah. Simeon and Anna waited their entire lifetimes for the advent of the Savior, holding onto promises from Jehovah God that they would see the Lord's Christ prior to their death. In the case of Anna, she lived twice the average life span of women of her day, and like Abraham and Sarah of old, she must have wondered at times if God would ever fulfill the promise—but her questions were those of faith ("How much longer?"), not unbelief ("Are you really going to…?").

Indeed, even wicked Herod, an apostate, blood-thirsty gentile believed the Magi's message that a new king was to be born. Herod wisely recognized events for what they were—special, historic—and acted cunningly to preserve his throne. And throughout the ministry of Jesus we see this divide between those who believe in the deity and saving work of Jesus, beyond all the limitations of this world, and those who make the choice not to believe. When doubters challenged Jesus for another sign or another miracle after all of his mighty works, he chided them that, "blessed are those who have not seen and yet have believed!"[21]

We are challenged by the example of Joseph: will we believe? Regardless of what we see in the disappointments and pain of this world, will we believe? There are many who believe that there is a God out there, somewhere, but due to bitterness, selfishness, pride, or disobedience refuse to act and acknowledge God's sovereignty in obedience. Joseph could have said, "What did I do to deserve all this trouble and the injury to my reputation?" Instead, he believed and accepted God's mysterious will,

---

[21] John 20:29.

with all of its troubles, for his life. Likewise, we are called on to believe and accept the will and way of God for our life, trusting that we will see the consummation of God's great plan unfold in our future.

Chapter 20

House of Bread

But you, Bethlehem Ephrathah, though you are small among the clans of Judah, out of you will come for me one who will be ruler over Israel, whose origins are from of old, from ancient times. Micah 5:2

The Gospel of Matthew reports that the religious leaders of Jesus' day knew that the Messiah would hail from Bethlehem. When the Magi arrived at Herod's court, with their tales of a supernatural star and a newborn king, the Jewish spiritual elite immediately quoted this passage from Micah, thus providing direction to the Magi and especially to Herod. Shortly thereafter, the Magi found the Christ there in Bethlehem, and the baby barely escaped Herod's murderous designs in subsequent days.

Bethlehem truly is the appropriate birthplace of the Savior. Bethlehem was the home to which Naomi returned with her widowed daughter-in-law Ruth. The latter married a prominent local kinsman named Boaz, and their great-grandson was David, slayer of Goliath, psalmist, and Israel's greatest king. Thus, Bethlehem is associated with the kingly tribe of Judah, King David himself, and we know from the genealogical prefaces to Matthew and Luke that Christ descended directly from David.

However, Bethlehem also symbolizes other features of Christ's person and ministry. Bethlehem means "house of bread" and "Ephrathah" means "fruitful." Although the town was not a great city, it was apparently rich in some agricultural resources. This association takes on a deeper significance when one considers that throughout Jewish history, bread has a larger symbolic and even mystical cultural significance. Anthropologists tell us that this has to do with the wonder that characterizes premodern societies' view that of natural, but seemingly supernatural, cycles of nature: the fertility process of the seed "buried" in the earth, the seasons, the harvest, and the like. This is a life-death-resurrection cycle that epitomizes God's creative order as well as the life and ministry of Christ.

Moreover, Jesus' ministry was routinely compared with that of Moses. It was Moses who led the people out of Egypt, gave them the Ten Commandments, shepherded them to the Promised Land, and through whom God provided food and water in the wilderness. Most notably, Moses was seen as the historic bread-giver, when God provided "manna" from heaven during the long exile in the Sinai desert.

Jesus himself was compared with Moses. In Matthew's Gospel, Christ is portrayed as the second law-giver, or better, the law-fulfiller. Matthew divided Jesus' teachings into five extended passages, analogous to Moses' five books of the Pentateuch (Genesis, Exodus, Leviticus, Numbers, and Deuteronomy). Some Jews accused Jesus of disrespecting and even breaking the covenant, but Jesus rejoined that he had come to fulfill the law of Moses.

Most obviously, Christ's miracle of providing bread to feed five thousand men and their families is foreshadowed by his birthplace, House of Bread, and directly associates him with Moses. In the Exodus account, Moses beseeched God to feed the people and God—not Moses—sent a bread-like substance from heaven called manna. In the story, it is clearly God who is the agent responsible for the miracle, not Moses.

In contrast, Jesus had his disciples seat a crowd of thousands and then blessed the lunch of a little boy that contained five loaves and two fishes. The miracle is well-known: not only was everyone fed, but twelve baskets of left-overs were collected. The miracle was so impressive that it was documented in all four of the New Testament Gospels.[22] This event was important because not only was Christ demonstrating his deity through a discrete miracle, but he was establishing a claim within the miraculous tradition of Israel's Jehovah utilizing the most humble and yet symbolically meaningful of miracles.

In John's Gospel, Jesus taught and even rebuked the people just a day after this miracle. He told them that he was the "Bread of Life," and that those who took him into their lives would never go hungry. The people, however, demanded a sign that he was the Son of God. Jesus recognized the challenge for what it was, and said to them, "I tell you the truth, you are looking for me…because you ate the loaves [yesterday] and had your fill…" In other words, they were following him around not to benefit from his teaching or to gain a closer relationship to God, but because they wanted him to meet their elemental needs for free. He challenged them, "Do not work for food that spoils, but for food that endures to eternal life."

Audaciously, the people challenge Jesus: "Our forefathers ate the manna in the desert…" and implied that Moses gave it to them. Jesus responded, "…it is not Moses who has given you the bread from heaven, but it is my Father…For the bread of God is he who comes down from heaven and gives life to the world." The people responded, "Sir, from now on, give us this bread."

So Jesus declared,

> I am the bread of life. He who comes to me will never go hungry and he who believes in me will never go hungry, and he who believes in me will never be thirsty. But as I told you, you have seen me and still you do not believe. All that the Father gives me will come to me, and whoever comes to me I will never drive away. For I have come down from heaven not to do

---

[22] Matthew 14, Mark 6, Luke 9, John 6.

> my will but to do the will of him who sent me. And this is the will of him who sent me, that I shall lose none of all that he has given me, but raise them up at the last day. For my Father's will is that everyone who listens to the Son and believes in him shall have eternal life, and I will raise him up at the last day.[23]

Jesus goes on in the following verses to again proclaim that he is the bread of life which brings everlasting life, in contrast with the manna of old which people ate, but was only temporary in its benefits: "Your forefathers ate the manna in the desert yet they died…I am the living bread that came down from heaven. If anyone eats of this bread, he will live forever." Finally, Jesus prophesied at this early stage of his ministry that he would give his life sacrificially at Calvary.

At the end of his ministry, Jesus once again took up this theme of living bread. In that instance, he was alone with his closest disciples and he bid them take and eat of the Passover bread, a memory of the Exodus, as a reconstituted symbol of deliverance—his very flesh that will be broken over the next day by beatings and crucifixion. Notice that the Bread of Life told his disciples to intimately sense the bread—to take it into themselves by eating it, not sniffing it, glancing at it, hearing it, or touching it: "Take, eat…"

This symbolism has been passed down to us through the centuries of Church history as the ordinance of communion. We are to take the symbols of Christ's flesh and blood, bread and wine, and ingest them into our innermost being. So too, we are supposed to accept and commit the person of Christ, the Living Bread, into our heart of hearts for spiritual renewal and vitality in this world and eternal life in the next. Hence, the symbols of life-giving sustenance—simple but essential life-giving bread—

---

[23] John 6: 35-40.

are found in Christ's ministry from his birthplace in the House of Bread to his ministry as the Bread of Life. That nourishing, healing, filling, and fulfilling Life's Bread is available to all today who are willing to accept Christ as the Son of God.

Chapter 21

The Historical Authenticity of Christmas

During the Christmas and Easter holidays each year, one of the major news magazines devotes a cover-story to the authenticity of Christ and his ministry. Usually the writer presents odd theories and ancient heresies about Jesus drawn from established myths and pseudo-scholarship. Nonetheless, the Christmas story does have a certain fantastic quality and Christians should not be timid in examining its historical reliability.

First of all, there continue to be those who suggest that Jesus never existed and that the four New Testament Gospels are historically suspect. This seems utterly ridiculous when one considers the evidence. Scholars suggest that the Gospel of Mark was written by Peter's apprentice John Mark based on Peter's eye-witness account within a decade or two of Jesus' death. Matthew and Luke were both white-collar professionals (a tax-collector/accountant and physician respectively), Matthew writing from personal experience and Luke drawing his from eye-witness testimony. The book of John followed sometime later, but again is based on his personal involvement in the details of the book. Indeed, these four eyewitness histories provide us with more direct evidence of the existence and about the person of Jesus Christ than we have for many ancient individuals.

It is worth noting that the historical and spiritual work that these men participated in did not win them earthly honors. Indeed church tradition asserts that they were all martyred for their faith; they so believed this "tale" of a virgin's offspring saving humanity that they refused to recant in the midst of terrible suffering. Luke may have been executed in Greece, Matthew in Ethiopia, Mark was dragged to death by horses in Egypt, Peter crucified upside-down in Rome, and after John survived boiling in oil, he was exiled for a time to the remote island of Patmos.

Despite widespread persecution, Christianity flowered in the century following Christ's death, providing us with numerous other believers who, despite the violent persecutions of Rome, believed the authenticity of the Gospel message as portrayed by the first apostles, including St. Justin Martyr (est. 100-165 A.D.), Polycarp (69-155 A.D.), Irenaeus (born about 115 A.D.), and a century later Tertullian (born about 167 A.D.) followed by the early church historian Eusebius (born about 260 A.D.).[24]

Christ's mere existence was also testified to by non-Christian sources as early as within the first century following his death. Among them was the Roman general, governor, and historian Cornelius Tacitus, who observed,

> But not all the relief could come from man, not all the bounties that the prince could bestow, nor all the atonements which could be presented to the gods, available to relieve Nero from the infamy of being believed to have ordered the conflagration, the fire of Rome. Hence to suppress the rumor, he falsely charged with the guilt, and punished with the most exquisite tortures, the persons commonly called Christians, who were hated for their enormities. Christus, the founder of the name, was put to death by Pontius Pilate, procurator of Judea in the reign of Tiberius, but the pernicious superstition, repressed for a time broke out again, not only in Judea, where the

---

[24] These dates are taken from a variety of sources on early Christian martyrs, but conform with those found at the online Catholic Encyclopedia, http://www.newadvent.org/cathen/05617b.htm.

mischief originated, but throughout the city of Rome also. (Annals, XV, 44).[25]

Other Romans also testified to the existence of Jesus Christ, such as Lucian of Samosata, the Roman historian Suetonius, the Samaritan historian Thallus, and Pliny the Younger, governor of Bithynia.[26]

Perhaps most important is the record by the famous, and infamous, Jewish general/historian/Roman collaborator Josephus. Josephus was the brilliant commander of the Jewish uprising that ultimately led to the destruction of Jerusalem in A.D. 70. Prior to Rome's crushing of the rebellion, Josephus changed sides. He wrote a monumental Jewish history that is still utilized today, despite its many limitations. Josephus wrote of Christ,

> Now there was about this time Jesus, a wise man, if it be lawful to call Him a man, for He was a doer of wonderful works, a teacher of such men as receive the truth with pleasure. He drew over to Him both many of the Jews and many of the Gentiles. He was the Christ, and when Pilate, at the suggestion of the principal men among us, had condemned Him to the cross, those that loved Him at the first did not forsake Him; for he appeared to them alive again in the third day; as the divine prophets had foretold these and ten thousand other wonderful things concerning Him. And the tribe of Christians so named from Him is not extinct at this day.[27]

Much more could be said that establishes the broader veracity of the New Testament and its relation to its historical context.

---

[25] Quoted in Josh McDowell's *A Ready Defense* (Nashville, TN: Thomas Nelson, 1992), p. 198.
[26] Ibid, 200.
[27] Antiquities, xviii, 33. Quoted in McDowell, 199.

For our purposes, however, it is clear that Jesus Christ was born to a Jewish family at the turn of the millennium and that his teaching and actions literally turned the world upside down. Moreover, following his crucifixion at the instigation of Jewish religious authorities, something happened that immediately transformed his ragtag band of followers into articulate zealots devoted to his teaching. They claimed to have seen a resurrected Lord. Furthermore, in one of Paul's letters in the second decade following Christ's resurrection, Paul reminds his readers that approximately 500 people saw the risen Jesus. Paul assumed that skeptics could travel to Judea and interview those eyewitnesses for themselves.

So what are we to make of Jesus? Beyond the ceramic babe that hides in our attic for eleven months each year prior to setting out our Nativity set, was this Jesus a real, flesh and blood infant and later man? Undoubtedly—he was a real person in history.

Second, what are we to make of his words and works: was he a good man, a teacher, a moralist, a criminal, a revolutionary? He said of himself, "I and the Father are one," and "I am the Way, the Truth, the Life..." He agreed when Pilate called him King of the Jews and asserted a heavenly kingdom. In sum, Jesus claimed to be God's son, divine himself, and therefore his voice confronts us through the ages: "Who do you say that I am?" Was he a liar? Was he a madman? Was he truly the Son of God?

The evidence of his life, miracles, teaching, and resurrection suggest that Jesus lived, died, and arose as God's only Son, Savior of the world, and that we can comfortably place our intellectual affirmation as well as our spiritual faith in his hands.

Chapter 22

Christmas is for Everyone

But you, Bethlehem Ephrathah, though you are small among the clans of Judah, out of you will come for me one who will be ruler over Israel, whose origins are from of old, from ancient times. Therefore Israel will be abandoned until the time when she who is in labor gives birth and the rest of his brothers return to join the Israelites. Micah 5:2-3

The first verse foretold that the Messiah would be born in the ancestral home of King David, Bethlehem. This firmly roots the Christ in the Jewish heritage. However, the second verse suggests that the fruits of the Savior's ministry were to be universal in scope and available to all men and women everywhere who accept Jesus Christ as Lord. Indeed, later verses speak of the Messiah's second coming when his "greatness will reach to the ends of the earth."

At the time of Christ's birth, Israel was abandoned, or better, Israel's apostasy distanced the Jewish people from God. Thus God left his people, living primarily in the two Jewish states of Israel and Judah, alone. God allowed both to be conquered by their neighbors as a consequence of their wickedness and idolatry. The northern kingdom of Israel was taken into captivity by the Assyrians in 722 B.C. and the southern kingdom of Judah was conquered by Nebuchadnezzar in 586 B.C. Although God allowed a remnant of the Jewish population to return, a period of 400 "Silent Years" followed: four centuries between the last Old Testament prophet Malachi and the coming of the Messiah's prophet John the Baptist.

Moreover, during the Silent Years the Jews did not exercise political sovereignty for long, but rather were caught up in the great games among empires of their day. They were first conquered by Assyrians and Babylonians and later absorbed into the Medo-Persian Empire. During all of this time, Israel was on the frontier between the Mesopotamian civilizations and the Egyptian empire, and thus was constantly in a state of uncertainty or war. In the fourth century before Christ, Alexander's armies defeated the Persians and claimed all of western Asia for Greece, but that empire fell apart into four sub-empires, Israel belonging to the Greco-Syrian realm of the Seleucids. It was a Seleucid monarch, Antiochus Epiphanes, who desecrated the Jewish temple by sacrificing a pig on the holy altar of Jehovah. Eventually, the Romans conquered the area and reigned during the birth of Christ.

This was the context into which John the Baptist entered to prepare society for Christ's entrance. John the Baptist brought a new day: the voice of God speaking directly after four centuries of pain and slavery. And of course the ministry of Jesus himself once again demonstrated the direct intervention of Israel's God in the Jews' affairs as well as his broader concern for humanity.

With Israel's years of captivity in mind, as well as Old Testament injunctions to holiness and separation from the sins of their neighbors, it was easy for the Jews to conclude that theirs was an exclusive God and that theirs was to be an exclusive Messiah. The verse from Micah means that nothing could be further from the truth. Micah prophesied that "the rest of his brothers return to join Israel." Some commentators believe that this fragment is referring to how, in the last days, a remnant of Jews will finally acknowledge Christ as Lord and turn their lives to him.[28] However, another interpretation lends itself.

---

[28] See Revelation 7:1-8.

Despite the antipathy Jews felt for gentiles in Jesus' day, a key theme of the Christmas story, and the later ministry of Jesus, is that God wants to reconcile everyone, not just the Jews, unto himself. Hence he brought foreigners (the Magi) to Jerusalem to witness to an Idumean king (Herod) and his pro-Roman court. This foreshadows Jesus' own ministry, which was primarily to the Jews but also reached aliens to the Jewish covenant. We have records of Jesus ministering to a hated Samaritan (Syro-Phoenician) woman, a representative of an apostate race. Similarly, Jesus healed the servant of a Roman centurion—the enemy occupier—and said the man had greater faith than anyone in Israel! We do not know how many other nationalities that Christ touched, but he also reached out to Jewish outcasts: lepers, prostitutes, and collaborators (e.g. tax collectors Zaccheus and Levi).

The message should have been clear: God's love is universal. The Bible story did not begin with a single chosen race, but with God seeking relationship individually with every man and woman. God's love was directly apparent to all three of Noah's sons, although apparently the descendants of Shem chose to stay closest to God. Likewise, Abraham's father and brethren all moved at God's call, but only Abraham obediently traveled all the way to the Promised Land. Other Old Testament patriarchs who begat Israel's neighbors, such as Lot (father of Ammon and Moab), Esau (father of Edom), and Ishmael (father of various Semitic peoples in Palestine and Arabia) all received direct testimony of God's desire to be in relationship with them.

The Old Testament story from Jacob/Israel on also advertises God's universal love. The Mosaic law allowed for gentiles to convert to Judaism, and there are numerous cases on non-Israelites who believed in the true God: Job, Rahab, Ruth, Namaan, and Moses' father-in-law the "priest of Midian." Similarly, God directly contacted many of Israel's neighbors with an opportunity for repentance and forgiveness, such as sending Jonah to Assyria's capital at Nineveh, Daniel to Babylon, and Elisha to the leaders of Syria.

The New Testament's emphasis on a universal gospel message is thus firmly rooted in the Old Testament. On the day of Pentecost, just a month following Christ's resurrection, the Good News was proclaimed to 5,000 Jews from around the world. Shortly thereafter Phillip converted an Ethiopian, Peter a family of Romans, and Paul began his famous missionary journeys throughout the Roman world. All of this was done to fulfill Christ's commandment, "Go into all the world and preach the Gospel…"

The apostle Paul later wrote, "For in Christ there is neither Jew nor Greek…" The point is that the Christmas message of a Savior's love is universal, not an exclusivist theme narrowly tailored within a distinctive cultural and ethnic tradition. It is the call for all of Israel's "brothers" everywhere to return to the true faith and be included as God's children in the kingdom of God.

The question for us this Christmas season is whether we live it so: are you and I taking Christmas global? Are we presenting Christ to all of our world? This includes our unsaved co-worker, our gay nephew, our Muslim neighbor down the street, the shut-ins, homeless, depressed, and lost. The joyous message of Christ's coming is designed to return all of these, and our own hearts too, to right relationship with God as his children and brothers in Christ.

Chapter 23

Doubt and Obedience

In the time of Herod king of Judea there was a priest named Zechariah, who belonged to the priestly division of Abijah; his wife Elizabeth was also a descendant of Aaron. Both of them were upright in the sight of God, observing all the Lord's commandments and regulations blamelessly. But they had no children, because Elizabeth was barren; and they were both well along in years. Once when Zechariah's division was on duty and he was serving as priest before God, he was chosen by lot, according to the custom of the priesthood, to go into the temple of the Lord and burn incense. And when the time for the burning of incense came, all the assembled worshipers were praying outside. Then an angel of the Lord appeared to him, standing at the right side of the altar of incense. When Zechariah saw him, he was startled and was gripped with fear. But the angel said to him: "Do not be afraid, Zechariah; your prayer has been heard. Your wife Elizabeth will bear you a son, and you are to give him the name John. He will be a joy and delight to you, and many will rejoice because of his birth, for he will be great in the sight of the Lord. He is never to take wine or other fermented drink, and he will be filled with the Holy Spirit even from birth. Many of the people of Israel will he bring back to the Lord their God. And he will go on before the Lord, in the spirit and power of Elijah, to turn the hearts of the fathers to their children and the disobedient to the wisdom of the righteous—to make ready a people prepared for the Lord." Zechariah asked the angel, "How can I be sure of this? I am an old man and my wife is well along in years." The angel answered, "I am Gabriel. I stand in the presence of God, and I have been sent to speak to you and to tell you this good news. And now you will be silent and not able to speak until the day this happens, because you did not believe my words, which will come true at their proper time." Meanwhile, the people were waiting for Zechariah and wondering why he stayed so long in the temple. ²²When he came out, he could not speak to them. They realized he had seen a vision in the temple, for he kept making signs to them but remained unable to speak. When his time of service was completed, he returned home. After this his wife Elizabeth became pregnant and for five months remained in seclusion. "The Lord has done this for me," she said. "In these days he has shown his favor and taken away my disgrace among the people."

In the sixth month, God sent the angel Gabriel to Nazareth, a town in Galilee, ²⁷to a virgin pledged to be married to a man named Joseph, a descendant of David. The virgin's name was Mary. The angel went to her and said, "Greetings, you who are highly favored! The Lord is with you." Mary was greatly troubled at his words and wondered what kind of greeting this might be. But the angel said to her, "Do not be afraid, Mary, you have found favor with God. You will be with child and give birth to a son, and you are to give him the name Jesus. He will be great and will be called the Son of the Most High. The Lord God will give him the throne of his father David, and he will reign over the house of Jacob forever; his kingdom will never end." "How will this be," Mary asked the angel, "since I am a virgin?" The angel answered, "The Holy Spirit will come upon you, and the power of the Most High will overshadow you. So the holy one to be born will be called the Son of God. Even Elizabeth your relative is going to have a child in her old age, and she who was said to be barren is in her sixth month. For nothing is impossible with God." "I am the Lord's servant," Mary answered. "May it be to me as you have said." Then the angel left her. Luke 1:5-38

The will of God is often obviously expressed in a manner that leaves no room for doubt as to how we are to respond. For instance, the Bible is full of clear injunctions and promises that delineate how one should treat God (love him with all your soul, mind, and strength) and others (love others, forgive them as Christ forgave you, do not steal).

In contrast, there are often huge differences in human reaction to the expression of God's will. In this passage there are two radically different responses to a direct revelation of God's will. Zechariah was burning incense in the holy temple of God. He was about as far removed from other humans as possible due to his purification for the ritual of bringing incense. Moreover, he should have been closer to God there—at the altar, expressing worship—than anywhere else on the planet. Thus it is entirely natural that he was astonished when another being joined him. To be fair, that being was the angel Gabriel, who regularly attended the very presence of the omnipotent God. Zechariah's reaction was more than surprise or shock. He was terrified ("gripped with fear").

Why was Zechariah frightened? The answer lies beyond being startled, which usually wears off quickly. In Zechariah's case, his fear may have indicated a pervasive spiritual doubt, dreariness, or even a mild (internal) rebellion caused by personal disappointment as well as the poor fortunes of his nation. Perhaps at that season of his advancing years Zechariah thought, "What's the use? The God in heaven doesn't seem to notice his people who have stumbled from one bad situation to the next, nor has he answered my petition for a son." Zechariah's focus on himself meant that his response to the angel was me-centered: "How can **I** be sure of this?"

Consider for a moment what Zechariah was saying. On the one hand, he did not dispute that this was a remarkable visitation. He did not question the credentials of the messenger. What he did reveal, however, was a smallness of spirit, bitterness, and a reservoir of doubt.

Indeed, Zechariah was so spiritually deadened and miserable over his own condition that he seemed not to have even heard the bigger story the angel had to tell. Gabriel said the child would have the spirit of Elijah and would prepare the way of the Lord! The birth of Zechariah's child was the minor miracle, harbinging the history-changing advent of the Savior of the world. Yet, Zechariah seems not to have noticed.

Zechariah did not acknowledge the coming of the Messiah. Instead, he murmured, "I am an old man and my wife is well along in years." His complete attention was directed at his own disappointments. He was well used to feeling sorry for himself.

When we focus our attention on God rather than ourselves—what he promises and desires—we will be more likely to respond as Mary did. When Mary was approached with the shocking news that she was to bear a child out of wedlock, she could have replied, "Haven't you considered my reputation?" She might have countered, "Can't we wait until after Joseph and I are wed? I promise to remain chaste." Mary could have responded, "How dare you make this decision without consulting me…it's my body…I did not ask for this!"

Perhaps these reactions do not fit Mary's character, but nonetheless in the moment of surprise she could just as easily have doubted God. She did not. Her attitude was, "I am the Lord's servant. Let it be to me as you say."

Interestingly, Mary was surprised enough and courageous enough to ask, "How will this be, since I am a virgin?" Unlike Zechariah, the attitude behind her question was neither doubting nor rebellious. Mary apparently believed the angel's message, but did not understand in the flesh how this could possibly occur. In good faith and curiosity she asked an obvious question, and was granted an answer.

Mary had enough faith and a good conscience that she went from the angel and told Joseph of God's promise that she would bear the Messiah. Obviously she explained that this meant she would be pregnant out of wedlock. Again, Mary must have been absolutely certain that she could trust the word of God, because she did what seems unthinkable in the natural—she told her fiancé that she was supernaturally pregnant.

Mary is a case in point of faith and obedience. She acceded to God's plan for her life. Her first words and later the Magnificat testify to her humility and sense of service to her Maker. Zechariah, in contrast, doubted the angel's word and was focused on his own limited horizon of hurt and disappointment.

For many people, the Christmas season has a way of drawing out an individual's disappointments about their life and relationships. The Biblical message is clear: we can humbly talk to God about how life has taken an unexpected turn or about a pain that tears at our soul. We would be in good company: with Abraham, David, Daniel, and even Jesus in the garden of Gethsemane. We can ask, "How can this be…" as Mary did. She did not doubt that God would fulfill his word, but she must have been anxious as to how Joseph would respond. How different though, is this than Zechariah's response, "What about me? What have you done for me? How can I be sure?" This Christmas holiday, if you have doubts, fears, or heartache, God stands ready to listen and bring new life where there was none before. By doing so, He will transform you and those around you.

Chapter 24

Troubled Jerusalem

After Jesus was born in Bethlehem in Judea, during the time of King Herod, Magi from he east came to Jerusalem and asked, "Where is the one who has been born King of the Jews? We saw his star in the east and have come to worship him." When Herod heard this he was disturbed, and all Jerusalem with him. Matthew 2:1-3

The court of Herod was a busy, bustling place. Although Herod was neither the most refined man of his day nor the most loved, he nevertheless was an engaged and exacting administrator. Herod was forever brimming with ideas for new projects which he hoped would buy him some affection from his subjects, and more importantly, stamp his name in history as a builder in the Roman mold. Herod's mind was also overflowing with conspiracy theories about how others were trying to take his life and throne. His delusions ultimately led to the execution, on charges of treason, of his beloved wife as well as some of his children.

Hence, it was probably not unusual for travelers of status to arrive on occasion at Herod's court, even in this Jewish backwater of the Roman Empire. Indeed, Judea was at the crossroads of East-West as well as North-South, and had long been traversed by caravanserai and fought over by empires.

But when the Magi arrived, they created uproar. We can assume this was not simply due to whom they were and what they represented, for it is possible that earlier eastern sages had crossed Judea en route to study in Alexandria or to embark from Caesarea for Athens or Rome. Of course, it is possible that the size or obvious wealth of the Magi's retinue, which could have been magnificent, may have caused some discussion. In any event, we know that what they had to say caused a disturbance.

One would expect that Herod, upon hearing from princely astrologers from Persia or Babylon that a new king had been born, would be "disturbed" or "troubled" (as the King James renders it) What is interesting, however, is that Matthew records that all of Jerusalem was troubled as well.

Why was this so? Why was it that the wise men's message started people talking across Jerusalem? What was it that worried, vexed, concerned, caused anxiety, and/or upset the population of the nation's capital?

The news, very simply, was of a new king. At first blush one would expect rejoicing from the notables of Jerusalem—a challenger was coming to topple the blood-thirsty, now-Jewish Herod and the pagan Rome he represented. But this was not the case—the people of Jerusalem were troubled.

Why? Certainly there must have been those for whom change of any kind would have been too much trouble. "The devil they knew" was good enough for them, and they finally were experiencing a bit of stability in their affairs, even if Herod was paranoid at times. But a new king...a new regime...a new way of doing business (both formally and informally)...new relationships—this portended discomfort at the very least.

Others were troubled because the very thought of the Magi's errand as supernatural put them in a state of denial. There were those who would not believe, could not bring themselves to believe, and therefore suffered from the emotional and mental anguish caused by cognitive dissonance. This condition seems strange, but how often do we turn our own backs on evidence that demands a verdict, such as a cheating spouse or a terrible medical diagnosis? The very presence of the wise men, who claimed to have followed a star 1000 miles or more, troubled these people.

A third group was troubled because the Magi's message defied religious convention. Were a king to come, they believed, he would be the son of one of the well-known Davidic families. Certainly Jewish leaders would have been told of his coming, not these heretics and sun worshippers! To the religious elite of the day, the Magi's errand threatened to disrupt the carefully cultivated Judaism which had survived the Babylonian captivity and the empires of the Persians, Greeks, and now Romans. Religion had been institutionalized around the new temple and its observances. There had not even been a Jewish prophet in 400 years. If what the Magi said was true, or worse, if it were believed by the simple and naïve, it could result in chaos and the destruction of the prevailing religious system.

Finally, there were probably those whose hearts were hardened to God and his plans, regardless of how those plans manifested themselves. This rebelliousness may have resulted from bitterness following loss, such as the death of a loved one or the dashing of great hopes. These might have once believed in the God of Israel, but felt he had abandoned them in their unique moment of need. Or those with hardened hearts may have been spiritually obtuse who spent their entire existence focused on personal comfort. Be they hedonists, gluttons, greedy, proud, or embittered, the Magi's words were unexpected and unwelcome.

Christmas has a way of disrupting our lives, just as it did in Herod's Jerusalem. It demands our thoughtfulness, forgiveness, charity, and patience while reminding us of past disappointments and hurts in an environment of hurry and stress. Christmas can be troubling, unless we listen for God's direction and embrace the message that a King has come to whom we must bow our will, our plans, our resources, and even our secrets. The wise men went on to find the child and "rejoiced with great joy," whereas Jerusalem was troubled and Herod angered. How will the challenge of Christ as King—of your time, talents, and money—affect you this holiday?

Chapter 25

God with Us

Therefore the Lord himself will give you a sign: the virgin will be with child and will give birth to a son, and will call him Immanuel. He will eat curds and honey when he knows enough to reject the wrong and choose the right. Isaiah 7: 14-15

All this took place to fulfill what the Lord had said through the prophet: "the virgin will be with child and will give birth to a son and they will call him Immanuel," which means, "God with us." Matthew 1:22-23

Matthew cites this passage from Isaiah as a prophetic announcement of the future Messiah's birth, pronounced seven centuries in advance. To Isaiah's hearers, the prophecy had immediate, local relevance. Little did they dream that these words were a double entendre—a reference to the coming Savior that asserts his humility of character and God's eternal promise to be available to His people.

Isaiah's prophecy was actually longer, and in its day was spoken directly to Judah's King Ahaz, a descendant of David. The political situation seemed dire, with Syria and the northern kingdom of Israel in league to attack Judah. Ahaz wanted to counterbalance their alliance by turning to the dominant power of the day, Assyria. In one sense, Ahaz had already surrendered to Assyria for he had rejected the God of Israel and worshipped idols like the Assyrians. Regardless of Ahaz's infidelity, God honored his promise to Ahaz's ancestor, David, to be Immanuel—God with us—to David's descendants in their time of peril, crushing both Syria and Israel within three years of the prophecy.

Matthew rearticulates Isaiah's prophecy to highlight the unique nature of Christ's birth: "a virgin shall conceive…" Again, however, it is the title that is pronounced that should be important to us: "God with us." The appellation characterizes the Messiah as one who came to live alongside his creation. Interestingly, the title says nothing about political dominion or military exploits, in contrast to the popular expectations of an apocalyptic Messiah which were current in Jesus' day.

This promise, that God will be with his people, echoes throughout the Biblical redemption narrative. God promised to be with Abraham, to be his "shield" and his "reward." God directly said, "I will be with you" to Moses, Joshua, and who knows how many other Old Testament heroes.[29] God saved his people countless times at the hands of Deborah, Gideon, Samson, and others as well as manifested himself physically to Shadrach, Meshach and Abednego in the fiery furnace and by a still small voice to Elijah when he was on the run. Most notably, Matthew records Jesus' last words to his disciples as, "And surely I am with you always, to the very end of the age."[30]

The Isaiah passage emphasizes the humanity of Jesus, a child eating "curds and honey." This is humble food, not the rich fare of royal banqueting halls, and some commentators suggest it symbolizes the uncertainty and nomadism of Christ's early childhood: the flight to Egypt and life as refugees in a foreign land. Joseph's family apparently lived in Egypt for some time, probably in humble circumstances, and then returned to Israel, again living in a parochial setting.

Not only was the fare of simple folk and travelers symbolic of Christ's early years, but it also tells us something about the nature of his adult ministry. There are those evangelists who

---

[29] See Exodus 3:12 and Joshua 1:15.
[30] Matthew 28:20.

seem to prosper in material possessions as their ministry expands. Jesus' experience was the opposite. He continued in penury throughout his ministry, once commenting, "Foxes have holes…but the Son of Man has nowhere to lay his head." In short, this Immanuel lived simply, as did the people he came to minister to. He came without pretension to trumpet the message of God's love for everyone, regardless of rank or wealth.

God promises to be present, to be with us. He sent his Son to live in the flesh: the Bible asserts that Jesus was fully human and even "tempted in all points" just as we are. Jesus knew hunger, thirst, persecution, disappointment, abandonment by his friends, betrayal, and temptation. Jesus experienced poverty. Jesus knew the loss of family, in fact, his closest cousin was beheaded by the king. Therefore, he knows precisely what it is to face limitation in this life, to experience disillusionment, to feel failure, to be disappointed. God did not promise to free us from the imperfections of this world. Rather, he promised to be with us as we live them, as Immanuel, God with us. This is a God who wants an intimate relationship with his creation and is willing to go to any length to make it happen.

Consequently, Christ is near at this very moment. He wants to be "God with us" to you and to your family. As in any other relationship, the choice is ours. Will you allow yourself to be comforted? Wooed? Befriended? Healed by the God who knows the number of hairs on your head? He is Immanuel, and wants to be *God with you.*

Reflection Questions

Chapter 1 – The Flight to Egypt

What personal sacrifices, if any, did Joseph and Mary make when leaving Bethlehem and then later Egypt?

While in Egypt, Mary and Joseph lived in one of the most cosmopolitan and wealthy areas in the world. Do you think it would be hard to leave Egypt to return to Nazareth, a rural backwater? Why/why not?

What lesson can you learn from Joseph's family leadership?

Discuss ways that our present day culture can hinder us from hearing God's voice and doing God's will.

Chapter 2 – Anna and Simeon

What did Simeon mean as he announced to Mary that a "sword will pierce your own soul?"

What message has God given to us regarding the counsel of our elderly saints of God? Can you think of an elderly person who has given you sound counsel? Have you thanked him/her?

The author notes that the Magi, shepherds, Mary, Joseph, Elizabeth, Zechariah, Simeon, and Anna were distinguished by their openness to God's leading and their willingness to follow. Write down a time when you knew God was speaking to you about a certain path to follow. Was it easy or difficult?

Chapter 3 – The Dedication of Jesus

What was the law concerning dedication of newborn male children (See Leviticus 12:4-6)?

What type of regulations or traditions do Christians practice regarding newborn children?

Compare the first covenant (given in Genesis) with the second covenant (Hebrews 9:11-15). See also scriptures on circumcision. Why is circumcision of the heart important?

Chapter 4 – Aunt, Mentor, Friend

What do we know about Elisabeth from the Bible? How do you imagine her?

How do you think Zechariah imparted his news to Elisabeth…as he was mute and perhaps deaf?

Elisabeth probably only influenced a handful of people during her lifetime, but among them were some key people: the mother of Christ, John the Baptist, and perhaps Jesus himself. Who is in your circle to influence?

Chapter 5 – Herod the Great

What did you learn about Herod? What surprised you?

Have you observed family characteristics and spiritual legacies—like that of Esau's family—in your own family or others? If the inheritance is a negative one, how can it be overcome?

There are numerous Old Testament prophecies about Edom's final destruction (Ezekiel 25:12-14, Ezekiel 35: 1-15, Amos 9:11-12, Isaiah 34:5-8). What are the characteristics of the Edomites that call for this judgment?

Herod the Great was a master builder, a cunning politician, and at times a deeply unhappy person. He seems to be entirely devoid of an interest in faith or spirituality. During the holiday season, are you more or less likely to be spiritually open and aware?

Chapter 6 – Jesus the Servant

Read Isaiah 42:1-4 as well as Matthew 12:15-24. What does the prophecy say about the Messiah?

In the passage from Isaiah, how can we reconcile the image that the Messiah would bring "justice to the nations" but that he would be so gentle as to not break a "bruised reed?"

Imagine that a young man that you know and had grown up with stood up in church one Sunday, read the passage from Luke 4 (see page 26), and announced that he was the Messiah. How would you respond?

In his announcement (Luke 4, cf. Isaiah 61), what did Jesus say his mission was?

Did Jesus fulfill this mission?

Chapter 7 – The Unexpected Christ

In what ways are the expectations of Christianity "unexpected" or surprising?

The Jews had suffered under the oppression of the Assyrians, Babylonians, Persians, Greeks, and Romans for 800 years, and it had been four centuries since the last prophet spoke to Israel. What kind of Messiah would the Jews have naturally wanted?

Why did God send Jesus as a servant rather than conquering hero?

Read the prophecy from Isaiah chapter 9 (page 29): did Jesus fulfill the prophecy? At his crucifixion, was he a disappointment to his supporters?

In your life, have you found Christ to bring any of the things mentioned in this passage?

Chapter 8 – Shepherds

Read the passage from Luke carefully: what specific actions did the shepherds do (clue: notice the verbs)?

What specifically did the angel tell them? Other than the angel's words, what other "message" did the angelic host convey?

How does God choose people to serve Him in specific ways? Has there been a time when you felt "called" to act in a certain way, or where – in retrospect – you realize that you were "in the right place at the right time" to serve God or others in some way?

Perhaps there were shepherds who heard the angelic message but did not make it to the manger – in your opinion, what kept them away?

Chapter 9 – What is in a Name?

What did you name your children? How did you choose their names?

In the Bible and in most traditional societies, the process of giving a name ("naming") has significance and even power attached to it. Those in authority such as parents or political leaders have the authority to name; so do masters over servants. Naming may be a testimony to past deeds may denote a future purpose. Which of these apply to God's naming of Jesus in today's text?

John the Baptist is the one other significant example of God naming someone at birth (Luke 1:13). Can you think of any other significant naming incidents in the Bible?

In Exodus 3:13-15 God self-identifies as "I AM." What is the significance of this name?

Why was Joshua a powerful Old Testament example for Jesus to be named after?

With this lesson in mind, what is the significance of Paul's writings on the "name of Jesus?" Paul routinely preached that "salvation came by no other name" but that of Jesus, such as in Philippians 2:9-11.

If your name, or reputation, is "Christian" (which means Christ follower, or Christ-like) – do you embody that name? Alternately, what "name" do people give you behind your back?

Chapter 10 – Jesus of Biloxi

Jesus grew up in a small town; what is small town life like? What are the strengths and weaknesses of growing up in a small community?

Imagine that a "prophet" or spiritual teacher showed up in Washington, DC or New York hailing from Biloxi (or Gallup or Arkadelphia or some other small town) ... and that he claimed to be the Son of God. How would you respond?

Jesus life was characterized by consistent, godly teaching, calls for repentance, and miracles. Did the fact that he had no money nor famous family connections help or hurt the credibility of his teaching and actions?

Jesus said that his teaching and his deeds were evidence enough that he was the Son of God. Put yourself in the place of first century

Jews: what evidence would be "enough" for you to accept Christ as Lord? What evidence do you need today?

Chapter 11 – The Light of the World

What are the properties of light the author uses to illustrate Christ's work?

How has Christ lightened or warmed your world?

What does scripture say about Christians being a light?

Chapter 12 – The Visitation of the Magi

Think of a time when you gave up comfort or safety to follow God's will. What was the end result?

What does each of the Magi's gifts symbolize? If you were the "fourth Magi," what would you have given in addition to these three gifts?

The author states that the Magi's anticipation of the King they would find differed from what they actually found: a small child born to poor parents. However, they were wise enough not to be disappointed. Discuss a time when following God's plan did not meet your expectations. How did you respond?

Chapter 13 – the Magnificat

What does Elisabeth say to Mary?

The following passages are referred to or are parallel to the Magnificat, which suggests that Mary knew the Scripture and that the Holy Spirit inspired her. Read the following verses and then read the

Magnificat: 1 Samuel 2:1-10, Psalm 138:6, Psalm 71:19, Psalm 126:2-3, Psalm 111:9, Genesis 17:7, Exodus 20:6, Psalm 103:17-18, Psalm 98:1-3, Psalm 118:15, Psalm 33:10, Isaiah 40:10, Isaiah 41:8-9.

What does the Magnificat tell us about God?

Chapter 14 – The Second Adam

What does it mean that God "breathed" into Adam and he became a "living being?"

In what ways are Adam and Jesus similar?

In what ways are Adam and Jesus different?

Chapter 15 – Zechariah's Prophecy and God's Mercy

What family names have significance in your family?

The neighbors asked Zechariah and Elisabeth two questions; what were they?

What are some of the symbols or Old Testament images (e.g. light) that Zechariah's prophecy associates with the Messiah?

How would you feel as a parent if God explicitly told you that your child would have a distinctive, high profile ministry?

What was John's mission to be?

Chapter 16 – The Genealogies of the Christ

What do you know of your own family tree? Do you have ancestors you are proud of? Who are famous? Who were outlaws?

In Jesus' genealogy, what names do you recognize?

Are you surprised by the names of Jesus' ancestors? Which ones, and why?

Read Ezra 9-10. The context is the Jews returning from captivity in Persia. Because these people who claimed to be priests could not verify their family records (genealogy), what did they lose?

What spiritual lessons should we draw from Jesus' genealogy about God's faithfulness?

If you were listed in an oral history/family tree that was handed down for generations – what would you want to be known for?

Chapter 17 – The Consolation of Israel

Why did Israel need "consolation?" What were they being consoled for?

Isaiah 40:1-5 gives a passage made famous in Handel's Messiah: "Comfort ye my people…" This foretells the coming of John the Baptist. How was John's message one of consolation?

Read Jesus' teaching from John chapters 14-16 on pp. 80-81? What does Jesus say that God's Spirit will do in the life of those who trust in Him?

How has God been a Comforter/Counselor/Helper to you? Are there areas where you need God's consolation at this point of your life?

Chapter 18 – Mary: Heroic and Human

If you are studying this as a group, read the passages from Luke as a dialogue: assign a narrator (the teacher), Mary, Gabriel, Joseph, and Elisabeth [Luke 1:26-38; Matt 1:18-25; Luke 1:39-54]

How do you picture Mary?

Note the order of events: it appears that the angel visited Mary, and then Mary (in Matthew) went to tell Joseph. It is only after Mary tells Joseph that the angel then visits Joseph. This was a courageous act on her part and it gave Joseph a chance to either join the salvation story, or bow out. At some point, Mary went to visit Elisabeth ... probably after telling Joseph [although this is not entirely clear]. What other choices did Mary have after the angel met her?

Joseph did not want to stone Mary; which was his prerogative under the law. Why not?

Why do you think that God chose Mary out of all the women in human history?

What does Scripture tell us about Mary?

Chapter 19 – Joseph the Dreamer

What characteristics did Joseph display that help us understand why God chose him to be Jesus' earthly father?

Review your list of characteristics. Examine your own life and compare with Joseph's. Which characteristic(s) are you lacking? Pray that God will help you develop in those areas.

This chapter indicates that Herod also believed the Magi's message. How is that someone can believe but reject Christ?

Chapter 20 – House of Bread

Bethlehem was the ancestral home of David's family. Does your family have such a center, a place where the family returns for vacations or to be buried?

In what ways was bread symbolic to people in Jesus' day? Does bread carry symbolism today?

Read Exodus 16:1-5, 13-15 and John 6:5-15. What are the differences and similarities between Moses and Jesus providing bread for the people?

Read John 6:25-66. What are the people asking for? What is Christ offering? Is some middle ground possible? Are the people being intentionally thick-headed in misunderstanding Jesus, or do they have some other motivations?

Do you have a testimony about Christ providing you the "bread of life?"

Chapter 21 – The Historical Authenticity of Christmas

Read Acts 1 and 2. What does Luke say about the authenticity of Christ's existence, particularly related to His resurrection?

Of what importance is there in an intellectual affirmation of Jesus' life, death, and resurrection? Isn't faith alone enough?

How can you use history to share the good news of Christmas with others?

Chapter 22 – Christmas is for Everyone

How was God reaching out to non-Jews in the Old Testament?

Some suggest that sharing Christian faith is cultural imperialism: is it? What is universal about the Christmas story and Christ's message?

The author asks us the question, "Are you and I taking Christmas global?" Think of someone who needs to hear the Christmas story. Pray for that person and pray for an opportunity to share the Christmas story with him or her.

Chapter 23: Doubt and Obedience

When you are startled or scared, what is your first reaction: fight or flight?

When Joseph heard the news of Jesus' birth, how did he respond? When Herod heard the news, how did he respond? Compare these with the responses of Mary and Zechariah to the angelic messenger.

Why do you think that Zechariah was terrified by the angel?

Do you think that the angel's response to Zechariah was unjust? Was his muteness punishment or a sign?

Mary questioned the angel, but unlike Zechariah was not punished for it. Why? What other Biblical figures questioned God? Is questioning God allowed?

Chapter 24 – Troubled Jerusalem

When you receive surprising news that may impact your family, how do you respond?

How do you think the Magi felt when they first became aware of the star and its significance?

Why were the people of Jerusalem troubled?

How has God challenged you at a time you were "troubled?"

How did the Magi respond when they came to the fulfillment of their journey?

Chapter 25 – God with Us

In what ways was Jesus "Immanuel" during his time of ministry here on earth?

What does "Immanuel" mean to you?

Reflect over the past year. List a time when you were disappointed, disillusioned, or felt abandoned. How did Christ manifest Himself as Immanuel to you?